United States Presidents

Dwight D. Eisenhower

D. Clayton Brown

Enslow Publishers, Inc.

40 Industrial Road   PO Box 38
Box 398   Aldershot
Berkeley Heights, NJ 07922   Hants GU12 6BP
USA   UK

http://www.enslow.com

Library of Congress Cataloging–in Publication Data

Brown, D. Clayton (Deward Clayton) 1941–
    Dwight D. Eisenhower / D. Clayton Brown.
      p. cm. — (United States presidents)
    Includes bibliographical references (p. 117) and index.
    Summary: Traces the life of the thirty–fourth president, from his
childhood in Kansas, through his military career, to his terms as
president and his efforts to preserve American strength during the
start of the Cold War.
    ISBN 0–89490–940–1
    1. Eisenhower, Dwight D. (Dwight David), 1890–1969—Juvenile
literature. 2. Presidents—United States—Biography—Juvenile
literature. [1. Eisenhower, Dwight D. (Dwight David), 1890–1969.
2. Presidents. 3. Generals.] I. Title. II. Series.
E836.B753   1998
973.921'092—dc21
   [B]   97–4368
                                  CIP
                                  AC

Printed in the United States of America

10 9 8 7 6 5 4 3 2

Contents

Major General Dwight D. Eisenhower (left) and U.S. Army Chief of Staff George C. Marshall (right) in 1943.

1

D-DAY: THE BATTLE OF NORMANDY

"O.K., We'll go." This statement, made by General Dwight D. Eisenhower, set into motion one of the greatest battles in World War II.[1] It was the famous D-day battle of June 6, 1944, the invasion of German-occupied France by Allied forces. The Allies, consisting of American, British, and Canadian forces, stormed ashore under heavy German fire. They established a beachhead that became the launching point for the destruction of Germany on the western front.

By giving this command, General Eisenhower sent twenty-three thousand airborne troops into German-held territory. They landed in specially built gliders or parachuted in during the night. They seized targets such as bridges and created confusion among the German troops. This strategy would help the main

Allied force landing on the beaches of Normandy, the French area on the English Channel and site of the battle.

Landing on the beaches was a combined force of over one hundred thirty thousand Allied troops. These fighting men, specially trained for this battle, had to endure some of the most deadly enemy fire of World War II. They were attacking the "Atlantic Wall," the heavily fortified defensive barrier built by the Germans to stop an Allied invasion. General Erwin Rommel was the German commander at Normandy.[2] He was highly respected by the Allied commanders. He was known as the Desert Fox because of his skill in fighting the Allies earlier in North Africa.

The D-day battle made General Eisenhower a world-famous figure. He was the Supreme Allied Commander and had the responsibility of organizing the 3 million men and women stationed in Britain to fight in World War II. General Eisenhower, known as Ike, faced one of the toughest choices of modern military history—and made the right decision. He had to decide if the invasion, the greatest amphibious operation in history, should go forward in a storm.

The invasion was very risky, even in good weather. It would be an amphibious landing, meaning troops would be ferried across the English Channel by ships, in the face of intense enemy fire. The beachheads, or the target landing sites, were code named. American troops were to land on Omaha and Utah beaches, and the

British and Canadians were to land on Sword, Juno, and Gold. The American beaches, especially Omaha, turned out to be the most heavily defended. German guns, some large enough to sink ships, were set in bunkers. German troops were stationed in underground bunkers and other defensive locations. Underwater mines and tank obstacles had been placed on the beaches. At the Omaha site there were bluffs or cliffs rising up from the beach.

Before the troops reached the beaches they would have to ride in specially built landing craft. During the battle, German gunners blew up some of the vehicles, but the Allied troops kept coming. When they reached the beaches, they had to run across an open area under heavy enemy fire. Eisenhower and his staff had worried that the losses among the soldiers would be high. There was even a serious question about using the airborne troops. One of Eisenhower's staff members estimated that as many as 70 percent of the troops might be killed or wounded in the battle.[3] One British general wrote: "It may well be the most ghastly disaster of the whole war."[4]

Even though Eisenhower had many generals and other advisors to help him with his responsibility, he had to make the final decisions. He, also, was worried about the battle, but he ordered his staff to be optimistic and to have faith in the plan. On the day of the invasion, however, he wrote a note to be released to the press if the battle failed. "Our landings . . . have failed . . . if any blame or fault attaches to the attempt it is mine alone."[5]

The D-day battle had been carefully planned. But the most critical factor in making the final decision was the weather—a storm blew into the English Channel on June 3, just before the battle was scheduled to begin. Crossing the sea and dropping airborne troops under the best circumstances was risky enough. When the weather turned sour, it put the whole battle, known as Operation Overlord, in jeopardy.

Weather had always been a special consideration. Conditions had to be just right. Glider pilots needed good visibility, and paratroopers jumping at night needed a full moon. Troops wading ashore during the day needed a low tide. Eisenhower had delayed the battle once due to a shortage of materials. During the period June 5–7, the moon and tide conditions were again favorable.[6] Now, another delay for any reason would seriously harm the whole secret invasion plan.

Eisenhower would have to wait until June 19 for the moon and tide to again be right for the invasion. By that time the Germans would likely have discovered the plan and reinforced their defenses. Another delay might demoralize the assault troops who were ready to go. The battle had also been timed to coincide with the start of a Soviet attack on the Germans on the eastern front. A delay could have serious political and military repercussions with the Soviets. On the other hand, if Eisenhower sent troops into battle during a storm, it could be a disaster. As Supreme Commander, he alone had to make the decision.[7]

For advice on weather, Eisenhower depended on British Captain John M. Stagg. With his staff, Stagg was responsible for providing the weather forecasts that were critical to the invasion decision. Stagg had accurately predicted that a storm would hit the English Channel on June 3. Eisenhower had temporarily postponed the invasion at that point and now waited for an improvement. Captain Stagg predicted that a lull in the storm would occur during June 5–6, but not all members of his staff agreed. Eisenhower now had to make a great decision based on a weather prediction that his meteorologists could not agree upon. Eisenhower wrote that "the weather in this country is practically unpredictable."[8]

Eisenhower called a meeting of his commanders at his headquarters. He asked for their advice. British Air Marshall Trafford Leigh-Mallory wanted another delay. He thought the weather was too poor for use of aircraft. Some members of his staff also recommended a delay. Others, however, urged him to go ahead, including British commander Bernard Montgomery. Eisenhower paced the floor. He would characteristically stick out his chin and ask for an opinion. The great decision weighed on him. "Probably no one," he wrote a short time earlier, "who does not have to bear the specific and direct responsibility of making the final decision as to what to do can understand the intensity of these burdens."[9]

After more thought he gave the famous command: "O.K. We'll go." His staff immediately ran out of the room and gave the orders to get the invasion started.

At this point Eisenhower was helpless. The battle was now in the hands of his soldiers. He could only wait as the greatest amphibious assault in military history went forward. He visited soldiers who were getting ready to embark on their mission. He held a press conference. About seven o'clock on the morning of June 6, he received news that the night landing of the paratroopers had succeeded. At that time, the landings of the troops on the beaches were underway.

The British and Canadians encountered light resistance at their beaches. For the Americans, under the command of General Omar Bradley, German resistance was stiff, particularly at Omaha Beach. Soldiers waded in chest-deep water, straight into German gunfire. Bodies of soldiers floated in the water and lay on the sand. It was here that bluffs arose from the beach, and the Americans took cover under them. If the soldiers moved they could be shot. Bradley considered withdrawing from Omaha. He knew, however, that it would jeopardize the whole invasion. He decided to slug it out. The U. S. Navy provided a heavy bombardment of the German defenses of Omaha Beach with its battleships and cruisers. Destroyers risked beaching in shallow water in order to get close enough to fire effectively on German targets. It made a difference. A report from V Corps, a unit fighting on the

In one of the most famous photographs of World War II, Eisenhower encourages the troops of the 101st Airborne Division as they prepare to invade France in June 1944.

beach, stated: "God bless the American Navy."[10] The troops began to rally and took the fight to the enemy.

In the meantime, progress was steady at Utah and the British-Canadian beaches. By the end of the day all beaches were secure. The next day, June 7, Eisenhower observed the battle site aboard the British ship *Apollo*. The landings were successful. A few days later he went ashore with Chief of Staff General George Marshall of the U. S. Army, who was Eisenhower's commander. Also going ashore with them were U. S. Navy Admiral Ernest

J. King and Army General Henry H. Arnold. With a sense of relief, Eisenhower and his fellow commanders ate lunch at Normandy, France.

Back in the United States, the American people reacted cautiously to the news of the invasion. As they realized that the Normandy invasion was the launching of the western or second European front, and that it was succeeding, they became more confident. In New York City, people attended special prayer services for the fighting men. In Philadelphia, the mayor ordered the Liberty Bell to ring for freedom. Eisenhower was featured in newspapers. His official news releases were printed in newspapers. He described the invasions as the beginning of a "great crusade" to free Europe.[11]

As the fighting continued, the Allied forces made slow progress. After approximately one month of fighting, the Allies broke through the German lines. Eisenhower's wisdom, and good luck, in deciding to attack on June 6 became apparent when a vicious storm struck the English Channel on June 19, the next time it would have been possible to invade Normandy. With the success of this great attack, Eisenhower became a world hero. His name was even mentioned as a future presidential candidate.

2

CHILDHOOD AND WEST POINT, 1890–1915

D wight David Eisenhower, the thirty-fourth president of the United States, was born in Denison, Texas, on October 14, 1890. His parents, David and Ida, met while attending Lane University in Kansas. They married in 1885. With his inheritance, David Eisenhower opened a general store in Hope, Kansas, a farming community near Abilene. They were prosperous, and their first child, Arthur, was born in 1886. But Eisenhower fell deeply into debt when a recession hit the area, and he lost his business. In 1889, while Eisenhower was traveling and looking for work, Ida gave birth to their second son, Edgar.

When Eisenhower found a job in Denison, Texas, working for a railroad, Ida joined him there with the two boys. Dwight was born during the short time they lived there. The family was poor, and when Eisenhower received an offer to work in the Belle Springs Creamery in Abilene, he accepted it. A relative of Ida's owned the creamery. The new job offered slightly more money. It also meant that David and Ida Eisenhower could live near their families. So in 1892 the Eisenhowers moved back to Abilene, Kansas. Dwight grew up there and always regarded it as his hometown.[1]

Abilene was the town on the north end of the famous Texas cattle drives. Before the Eisenhowers' ancestors moved there from Pennsylvania in 1878, it was famous for gunfights among cowboys. During Dwight's childhood it was an isolated town on the Kansas prairie and no longer had cowboys and gunfights. There were stories about Wild Bill Hickock, who had been the marshall of Abilene for a short time in 1871.[2] The town had a small population of only several hundred. It served the farmers in the area and had a depot on the Union Pacific Railroad. For several years after the family moved back from Texas in 1891, the streets were not paved. It had only one policeman and three schools. There were many churches, and for most families, social life revolved around them. The shops and stores were not fancy. After he became president, Eisenhower described his hometown as "peaceful and quiet."[3]

Nearly all the people of Abilene had to work hard. Dwight's father was a mechanical engineer who repaired equipment in the town's creamery. The family kept growing. David and Ida Eisenhower had four more boys: Earl, Roy, Paul, and Milton. In 1896 Paul died of scarlet fever at the age of two. The family had to watch expenses. All of the boys stayed busy by helping at home and working at part-time jobs when they were not in school. Each son had a small plot in the family garden. All of them raised vegetables and sold them to the townspeople. Dwight learned to work early in his life and to be careful with his money.

Dwight was a bright child who made good grades. He was full of energy and grew accustomed to staying busy at an early age. He used to make extra money by cooking tamales and selling them to townspeople. He sold three tamales for five cents, and if there were any leftovers, Dwight and his brothers quickly ate them.[4]

Dwight grew up in a close and affectionate family. His father spent long days at the creamery and his mother managed the house—and the six boys. Dwight's grandfather also lived with them. They had regular prayer each day, and the family had a Bible-study session usually once a week. As soon as each child could read, he had to read passages from the Bible to the family. The Eisenhower boys could quote chapter and verse from the Bible. By sharing responsibilities such as gardening and numerous household tasks, the children participated with their parents in maintaining the home. The Eisenhowers were a happy and devoted family, and when he was president, Eisenhower fondly

Eisenhower's fifth-grade class in Abilene, Kansas. He is second from the left in the front row.

remembered his childhood in the house on Fourth Street in Abilene.

The Eisenhower family lived on the south side of town, across the railroad tracks that separated them from the nicer homes. A sense of rivalry existed among the children on the two sides. Fights naturally broke out. Dwight's older brother Edgar was known as Big Ike. Dwight was known as Little Ike. Dwight was later called just Ike. It was a name that stayed with him for the rest of his life. On one occasion Dwight fought a particularly tough, and larger, boy from the other side. Dwight was at a disadvantage, but he fought until the other boy agreed to quit. It was described in one account as "an epic of brutal courage."[5] The Eisenhower boys often had to wear hand-me-down clothes, and when other children ridiculed them, they fought back.

At that time, education was not as highly valued as it is today. David and Ida insisted, however, that their sons go to school. When Dwight enrolled in the first grade, there were about two hundred children in his class, but only thirty-one of them finished high school. Dwight enjoyed reading and was fond of history. The practice of Bible reading at home helped him in school, but his best subject was geometry. One year the teacher let him work the geometry problems without the use of a textbook.

Though Dwight was a good student, he had to repeat one year because of a severe illness. When he was fourteen and in the ninth grade, Dwight fell and skinned his knee while playing with some friends. The next day, after school, he was delirious with pain and his leg was swollen. His parents had a doctor examine him. Dwight thought the doctor wanted to amputate his leg. Dwight wanted Edgar to stay in the bedroom and keep the doctor away. His mother and one of her friends, however, nursed him.[6] Hoping to keep the infection from spreading, the doctor painted carbolic acid, a strong disinfectant used in surgery, around his leg and groin. It worked. A few days later, Dwight started improving and the swelling began to disappear. The incident cost him about two months of school, and he had to repeat the ninth grade.

Eisenhower's letter to his cousin, written on February 27, 1905. In it he explains he had been sick and apologizes for not writing sooner.

spelling to for all of that, Roy and I have baked pies three times and a lady baked some for us an my cousin baked i for us today well write soon even if I don't do it mysel it is 3 weeks today since Milton took sick from your cousin

D. Dwight Eisenhower,
201 S. S. 4th st,
Abilene, Kansas.

P. S. That picture was a pretty one.

Although Dwight was busy with schoolwork and home chores, plus working at small jobs, he enjoyed himself. He went hunting, fishing, and camping with his friends. It became customary for him to serve as the cook when he went camping with his friends, and for the rest of his life he enjoyed outdoor cooking. Dwight liked sports, particularly baseball and football, and played on the school teams. At the age of fifteen he learned to play poker from Bob Davis, an illiterate man who lived on the Smoky Hill River near town and earned his living by fishing and trapping. The town's boys admired Bob Davis. Dwight became an excellent

Eisenhower in 1904, enjoying one of his favorite boyhood activities—camping with friends.

player, learning to use patience and to understand all the options available to him. He applied these poker-playing skills throughout his career.[7]

When he graduated from high school in 1909, he wanted to go to college. His brother Edgar wanted to go to the University of Michigan, so Dwight and Edgar made an agreement. They would work and put each other through college because their parents could not afford to send them. Dwight agreed to stay home since he was younger and work to support Edgar. At the end of a year, it would be Edgar's turn to support Dwight if it were still necessary. This arrangement lasted for about a year until Dwight Eisenhower was accepted to West Point, the United States Military Academy.

During that year he worked at several jobs, always moving to a new job that paid more money. First he worked on a farm and then for a company that made metal grain-storage bins. He then went to work at the creamery, keeping long hours and working at night. By then, Eisenhower wanted to start college himself, so when his friend Everett (Swede) Hazlett suggested that Eisenhower try to get into the U. S. Naval Academy with him, he eagerly accepted the idea. They studied together in order to take the qualifying examinations, and they both scored well on the tests. But Eisenhower could not attend because there was an age limit on new students. He would be twenty-one years of age when he started at the Naval Academy, so he was ineligible. This realization came as a great disappointment to him, but he decided to try to get into the Army's academy at West Point. After taking another series of qualifying tests, Eisenhower received an appointment to West Point from Kansas Senator Joseph Bristow in 1911. This was the beginning of his military career.[8]

Eisenhower had not planned on a military career, but he was delighted to receive the appointment because it meant a free college education—a serious consideration for a large family. As he prepared for the train trip to West Point, he sensed the importance of his departure. He realized it would mean a change in his

The circus dog Flip poses in 1910 with (left to right): Eisenhower's brother Milton; his father, David; Dwight (the tallest); his mother, Ida; and brother Earl.

life, that he was leaving behind his parents, brothers, and hometown. He would miss his dog, Flip, who had been a circus dog and could jump through hoops and stand on his hind feet. Eisenhower had been happy at home, but he knew that his childhood had passed. On the day he left, his mother cried, something none of the boys had ever known her to do.

His experience at West Point was, of course, an important part of his life. Eisenhower was a good student. His disciplined life and hard work in Abilene made West Point easier for him. Some of the cadets could not withstand the pressure. About fifty of his classmates dropped out by the end of the first year, including his own roommate. But Eisenhower's grades were good and his overall rank for the first year was 57th out of 212 students. Eisenhower also enjoyed himself and received a lot of demerits for pranks and mischief. Demerits were given to students for breaking rules. Demerits had to be removed by performing extra assignments such as guard duty. He would wear the wrong uniform to drill practice or be late for meals. In one instance during his senior year, he received demerits for dancing too wildly at a school dance in spite of an earlier warning.[9]

Eisenhower played on the West Point football team. It was the most enjoyable part of his four years at the academy. He took football more seriously than his studies. Dwight played running back behind the team's star, Geoffrey Keyes. Once, when Keyes was injured, Eisenhower played for two games. He ran well and

Eisenhower in his full-dress uniform at West Point in 1911.

received much praise for his game. When Keyes came back after his injury, Eisenhower still substituted for him and again played well. During the game against Tufts University, Eisenhower twisted his knee. He seemed to have recovered, but a short time later he renewed the injury during a horseback-riding drill and had to be hospitalized for four days. He could no longer play sports. Eisenhower was greatly disappointed, because football meant a lot to him. For a while he was depressed and thought about leaving West Point.[10]

At the end of their second year, the cadets were allowed a thirty-day furlough to go home. Eisenhower went back to Abilene and saw his family for the first time since he had left two years earlier. His family and friends were proud of his work at West Point, and Eisenhower was proud of himself. On some days he wore his cadet uniform in town so that people could see him in it.

When he returned to West Point, he remained active in school affairs, even though he could not play football. He became a cheerleader and one of the color sergeants. Eisenhower continued to receive demerits for his rebellious behavior. He started smoking cigarettes, and although cigars and pipes were allowed, cigarettes were not. He did not worry about his demerits. "I enjoyed life at the academy," he later wrote, "had a good time with my pals, and was far from disturbed by an additional demerit or two."[11] His grades never suffered because of his pranks. He could write an English

Dwight D. Eisenhower

SOURCE DOCUMENT

EXTRACTS FROM RECORDS OF CADET DWIGHT D. EISENHOWER, USMA, 1915

D. D. Eisenhower
Appointed Corporal 12 June 1912 by USMA Special Order 121, dated 12 June 1912.

Appointed Sergeant 12 June 1913 by USMA Special Order 103 of 12 June 1913.

Punished by Special Order No. 106, 16 June 1913.
"Violation of orders in reference to dancing, having been previously admonished for same offence", 11th instant, his appointment as Sergeant was revoked and from Sept. 1 to 30, 1913, he will be confined to the barracks, area of barracks and gymnasium and will serve punishment tours every Wednesday and Saturday at prescribed hours.

Delinquencies for Cadet Dwight D. Eisenhower taken from Abstract of Delinquencies from 15 July 1911 to May 1915.

1911 (4th Class)

15 July	Relieved from post by permission at 7:35 a.m., 11th instant (no delinquency). Orderly board not properly posted during parade, July 14. 1 demerit. Tarnished rod in cartridge box at parade. 1 demerit.
20 July	Absent at 8 a.m. drill formation. 3 demerits.
30 July	Overshoes not arranged as prescribed at retreat. 1 demerit.
2 August	Dirty gun and collar not properly adjusted at parade. 4 demerits. Overshoes not in prescribed position during parade. 1 demerit.
10 August	Late at 7:05 drill formation. 1 demerit.
13 August	Late at chapel. 1 demerit.
27 August	Falling in without waist belt when the guard was turned out 1:15 p.m., Aug. 26. 2 demerits.
3 September	Late at parade. 1 demerit.
7 September	Room in disorder, afternoon inspection. 2 demerits.
12 September	White trousers on chair, afternoon inspection of barracks. 1 demerit.
17 September	Late at guard mounting, Sept. 16. 1 demerit. Bedding not properly arranged, S.M.I. 1 demerit.
18 September	Section marcher, dismissing section before it was opposite door of first division. 2 demerits.
22 September	Late at breakfast. 1 demerit.

Taken from official records of West Point Military Academy, 1915, this page shows examples of cadet Eisenhower's demerits and the reasons for receiving them.

paper in thirty minutes, whereas his friends agonized over one for several days. Later in his career Eisenhower was well known in the Army for his ability to write and organize reports. He continued to excel in geometry, and in one class solved a long problem in such a short time that the mathematics department taught his approach to the problem in other classes.[12]

When he graduated in 1915, he almost did not get recommended for a commission because of his knee injury. He promised the examining physician that he would ask to be assigned to the infantry if it would help him stay in the Army. So, Dwight D. Eisenhower was commissioned a second lieutenant in 1915. He went home to Abilene for a short visit until he received his orders to begin active duty. In September 1915, he reported to the 19th Infantry Regimental Headquarters in San Antonio, Texas.

3
MILITARY
CAREER, 1915–1941

In September 1915, when he was twenty-four, Eisenhower arrived at Fort Sam Houston in San Antonio. He assisted in training troops. He had some extra time during the afternoons, enough for him to coach football at the Peacock Military Academy. He still enjoyed the sport and was happy to serve as the coach. He met his future wife, Mamie Geneva Doud, who was nineteen, on a Sunday afternoon in October on the Army base. He was making his rounds as Officer of the Day, which required him to make inspections of the base. Mamie lived in Denver, Colorado, with her parents, who came to San Antonio each winter to escape the cold weather. On that day, Mamie was sitting outdoors with a group of women, visiting a family friend, Mrs. Lulu Harris. Mrs. Harris asked Eisenhower to come over and meet some of her friends. He refused at first, but Mrs. Harris persuaded him to stop long enough for introductions.

He was impressed with Mamie and asked her to accompany him on the rest of his rounds. She accepted. "I never walked so far in my life," she later recalled.[1] The next day he called her, asking for a date. She said she was busy, but he kept asking when she would be free until she agreed to see him, four weeks later. They started seeing each other. She enjoyed watching him coach the Peacock football team during the afternoons. They were happy together and got married on July 1, 1916, at her parents' home in Denver.[2]

The days of relaxation did not last long. World War I had started in Europe in 1914, and the United States entered the war in 1917. For Eisenhower and other officers, it was an opportunity to gain combat experience and advance their careers. He applied for transfer to Europe, but he was assigned to an Army base in Georgia to help train officers. Mamie stayed in San Antonio. At this time, she had their first child, Doud Dwight, who they nicknamed Ikky.[3] Eisenhower continued to request transfer to Europe but was sent to Camp Colt, a tank training school at Gettysburg, Pennsylvania.

At Camp Colt, Eisenhower was busy. Again he assisted with troop training and working out tactics for tank maneuvers. Sometimes he had to procure supplies for his men. He was delighted when, in October 1918, he received orders to go to Europe. The war ended the next

Lieutenant Eisenhower and his new bride, the former Mamie Geneva Doud, in San Antonio, Texas, in 1916.

month, however, and his orders for duty in Europe were canceled. Eisenhower was greatly disappointed that he had not had the chance to command troops in battle.[4]

When the war was over, most young men sought careers in business. The United States had little interest in foreign affairs, and the Army and Navy were kept small because few people expected the country to go to war again. Careers in the military were not popular, because promotions, based on seniority, came slowly. Also, jobs and careers in the civilian sector paid better. Eisenhower stayed in the Army and never regretted his decision. He refused to consider offers to work in another career.

He remained devoted to the Army and received valuable experience. In 1919 he was stationed at Fort Meade, Maryland, where he experimented with a new weapon, one that Eisenhower was sure would be important in the next war, whenever it came. The new weapon was the tank, and here he met a young officer who was also experimenting with tanks. They became close friends and together produced some of the Army's basic maneuvers in tank warfare. The officer was George Patton. Both of them believed in the swift movement of armored vehicles—and they believed in military air power, another warfare innovation pioneered during World War I. Eisenhower and Patton were young officers who were certain warfare had changed dramatically, that it would no longer be slow and cumbersome, but fast, incorporating the use of tanks and aircraft.[5]

Eisenhower at Fort Meade, Maryland, in 1919, where he developed tactics for tank warfare.

One night he and Mamie were visiting Patton and his wife, Bea. They met General Fox Conner, a dinner guest of the Pattons'. Conner had served on the General Staff of the Allied Expeditionary Forces in World War I. Conner was impressed with Eisenhower's views about the use of tanks in warfare.

While Eisenhower was at Fort Meade, he and Mamie often hosted parties at their home. Mamie, who could play the piano, led the singing, and her husband excelled at playing cards. They were popular and their home was known as Club Eisenhower. Ikky was popular, too, and received much attention. He was declared mascot of the corps. In December 1920, Ikky caught scarlet fever and died a short time later. He was only three years old. His death deeply hurt Mamie and Ike. Each year for the rest of his life, Eisenhower sent Mamie a bouquet of roses on Ikky's birthday, even when he was stationed away from her.[6]

In 1919, Eisenhower was part of a special cross-country trip conducted by the Army with trucks, an experiment in the movement of men and supplies. The trip took two months. It went from Washington, D.C., to San Francisco. Often the convoy had no road to follow. Trucks broke down every day and progress was slow. Usually they traveled about forty to fifty miles per day, or even less. This trip made him understand the importance of good roads and of the need for efficient ways to move military supplies.

In 1920, General Conner was put in command of the

20th Infantry Brigade at Camp Gaillard in the Panama Canal Zone. He asked Eisenhower to serve as his executive officer. Eisenhower accepted the offer, but his commanding officer at Camp Meade, General Samuel Rockenbach, refused to give him a transfer. Eisenhower was coaching the football team at Camp Meade, and Rockenbach did not want to lose him. About a year later, however, Eisenhower finally got the transfer. Mamie finally thought Panama would be fun. They moved to Panama in January 1922 and lived there for two and one-half years.

General Conner had a great impact on Eisenhower. Conner was convinced that another major war was coming and that Eisenhower should prepare for it. Under his guidance, Eisenhower studied military, political, and economic affairs of the world. They had many long discussions. Because of this experience with Conner, Eisenhower had a better understanding of the world and its history. He was already known as a good writer and organizer. Now, with the influence of Conner, he started to become a thinker and strategist. Conner told him about George Marshall, who was known as a rising star and one of the ablest men in the Army. Marshall became the Army Chief of Staff during World War II and had a critical role in shaping Eisenhower's career. Later, Eisenhower described his assignment in Panama with Conner as a "graduate school."[7]

While they were stationed in Panama, the Eisenhowers had their second child, a boy named John.

It was a great moment for them. John brought much love and joy into their lives and helped them cope with the loss of their firstborn.

In 1924, when his duty was finished in Panama, Eisenhower received orders to return to Camp Meade in Maryland. His job: to coach the football team. This assignment made him angry because he did not want to continue coaching. "Someone in Washington," wrote one historian, "had decided that the Army needed to beat the Marines. . . ."[8]

Eisenhower still loved football but did not want it to interfere with his professional career. Nevertheless, he returned to Camp Meade and coached. He then requested to be sent to the Army Infantry School. His request was denied. With the help of General Conner he was sent to the Army Command and General Staff School, where the finest officers and future commanders received special training. He worked hard while in the school and graduated in 1926 at the top of his class. Eisenhower had proved that he was very intelligent and hardworking. His years of work at home and school as a child in Abilene had given him the discipline needed to excel in such a competitive school.[9]

Upon graduation from the U.S. Army Command School, he started receiving important assignments. General John Pershing, the famous commander of American forces in World War I, requested that Eisenhower be assigned to the Battle Monuments Commission. Pershing had organized the commission and wanted Eisenhower to record the histories of the major battles in World War I.

Eisenhower had worked with General Pershing for only a short time when the Army gave him the chance to attend its War College in Washington, D.C. He went to the college for about one year. It was not demanding: Students listened to lectures about government and military affairs. When Eisenhower finished, Pershing wanted him back to finish the histories for the Monuments Commission. Mamie urged him to accept Pershing's request because it would enable them to live in France. He accepted the new job. It kept him back in contact with Pershing and gave him a thorough firsthand knowledge of the terrain and geography of France.

Once he finished his assignment to the Monuments Commission, Eisenhower and his family returned to the United States. He was now on the fast track of highly important assignments, including some that gave him contact with political and economic leaders. In 1929 he was thirty-nine. At the rank of major, Eisenhower was transferred to the office of Assistant Secretary of War in Washington, D.C., where he worked on plans for industrial wartime mobilization. He reported to General George Van Moseley. His work on mobilization started in 1929 during the Great Depression, a period of poor economic conditions and high unemployment. In this position he learned a lot about political affairs in Washington and worked with some very powerful people, including Bernard Baruch, the famous industrialist.[10]

In 1930, General Douglas MacArthur became Army Chief of Staff. He made Eisenhower his aide. In July 1932, Eisenhower was involved in the Bonus Army march in Washington, D.C. This march resulted because, in 1924, the government had arranged to provide payments to the veterans of World War I on a yearly basis for the next twenty years. They started receiving some money each year. In 1932, however, the veterans wanted to get the rest of their money in advance. Many of them were unemployed due to the poor conditions of the economy. In order to persuade Congress to authorize the early payment, veterans marched to Washington. About two thousand of them stayed in tents and shacks in the city. They were peaceful and did not pose a threat.[11]

At that time, the president was Herbert Hoover. He became convinced that the veterans were dangerous. He ordered the Army to expel them from the city and return them to their camps outside the city.[12] General Douglas MacArthur personally took command of the evacuation. He ordered Eisenhower to accompany and assist him. The veterans were driven out of the city by Army troops. Furthermore, MacArthur disobeyed the president's commands and drove the veterans out of their camps outside the city. Their tents and shacks were burned to the ground, and tear gas was used to force them to leave. Some were injured. Hoover was severely criticized for the incident. Eisenhower was sympathetic toward the veterans and did not approve of MacArthur's handling of the evacuation. He insisted, however, that the evacuation had been a political decision.[13]

A few months later, in January 1933, Eisenhower became MacArthur's personal military assistant. In this position he continued to meet important people, including members of Congress and some who worked with the new president, Franklin D. Roosevelt. Eisenhower, by now a colonel, helped MacArthur with some of his most important work, such as preparing material for the president and for Congress. In 1934, MacArthur was assigned and sent to the Philippines as military advisor.

Located in the Pacific Ocean, the Philippine Islands belonged to the United States. The U.S. government had given them commonwealth status in 1935, which meant they would be a self-governing territory associated with the United States. In 1946, the Philippines would be completely free. MacArthur asked Eisenhower to continue serving as his personal assistant. Eisenhower wanted to command troops, but he could not refuse the Army Chief of Staff, and he spent the next four years in the Philippines.[14]

As MacArthur's aide, Eisenhower had a large role in organizing and training the Philippine military forces. He worked closely with Philippine president Manuel Quezon. Eisenhower helped develop their air force and learned to fly an airplane himself. The resources for the defense of the islands were limited, and he knew they could not withstand an attack by a major power. With his assistants, Eisenhower worked hard to improve the Philippine defenses. During his assignment in the Philippines, he learned a lot about government. He held long discussions with President Quezon about taxes, schools, finances, and other topics. In this respect, his experience with the Philippine president resembled his association with General Conner.

The Eisenhowers stayed busy while they lived in the Philippines. Mamie was happy to be with her husband, and John went to high school there. John and his father spent time together, hiking through the jungles and enjoying themselves in other outdoor activities. Their home, a luxurious apartment, was a central point for entertaining high-ranking political and military officials.[15]

Eisenhower (in center, wearing white suit) with members of the Philippine Air Force in 1939.

Their lives, like those of people around the world, started changing in 1939, when war broke out in Europe. The United States faced danger in Europe, where Germany was at war with Great Britain and France. In the Pacific the Japanese were belligerent. They sank an American ship, the *Panay*, in 1937, and violated American rights in China in 1939. By that time Eisenhower was convinced the United States would be drawn into the European war. He asked to be sent back to America to command troops.[16] In late 1939, the Army assigned him to be the executive officer at Fort Lewis, Washington. John had finished high school and decided to attend West Point. In 1940, Germany and Japan signed the Tripartite Pact, an agreement that promised they would help each other if either one of them got into war with the United States. Eisenhower fully expected the United States to be at war soon.[17]

He enjoyed being with the troops at Fort Lewis, but he spent only a short time there. A significant change came in June 1941, when he was reassigned to Fort Sam Houston in San Antonio, where he and Mamie had met in 1915. They looked forward to returning to San Antonio, a city that Mamie loved. He was now the Chief of Staff of the Third Army. Colonel Eisenhower received a special task: He was to organize and conduct the largest peacetime training exercise in American history. He had to conduct a war game with three hundred thousand troops in Louisiana. The Army wanted to work out its command system and provide combat-like experience for its soldiers. It was an important exercise for Eisenhower—and for the United States. Patton also participated. It was a great success. Army officials were impressed with the training exercise and praised the work of all the officers in it. Eisenhower was promoted to Brigadier General.[18]

He returned to San Antonio and continued to work very hard. On Sunday, December 7, 1941, he took a nap in the afternoon and asked not to be disturbed. One of his officers, however, called him on the telephone.[19] The Japanese had attacked the United States at Pearl Harbor, Hawaii, without warning, killing about two thousand Americans and destroying ships, aircraft, and buildings. The next day, President Franklin D. Roosevelt asked Congress for a declaration of war against Japan. A few days later Germany declared war on the United States. The hardworking and happy child of Abilene was poised for the greatest war in American history. Eisenhower remembered the advice of General Conner, who believed another major war was coming. He had warned Eisenhower to prepare for it.[20]

4

WORLD WAR II

In 1941 the United States faced one of the greatest wars in its history. It had to fight Japan in the Pacific and Germany and Italy in Europe. These three countries were known as the Axis powers. Germany, controlled by the Nazis, held nearly all of Europe. Japan already held some major areas in Southeast Asia, and it was expanding throughout the Pacific. Only a few days after the Pearl Harbor attack, Japan invaded the Philippines, where Eisenhower had lived for four years. It continued to conquer other countries in Southeast Asia. Along with the United States, other countries were fighting the Axis powers. They were known collectively as the Allies. America's best-known Allies in the European war were Great Britain and the Soviet Union. President Roosevelt and his top military advisors had to decide the best way to fight the war. The Army Chief of Staff in Washington, D.C., was General George Marshall, and the president depended on him for answers.

In San Antonio, Eisenhower received a telephone message from General Marshall a few days after the Pearl Harbor attack. The order was brief but clear: "The Chief says for you to hop a plane and get up here right away."[1] Eisenhower and Mamie canceled a trip to visit their son at West Point. Eisenhower left immediately. Mamie stayed in San Antonio.

The United States was not prepared for war. When Eisenhower walked into the Chief of Staff's office a few days later, Marshall asked him to prepare immediately a plan for fighting the Japanese. Within a few hours Eisenhower had a strategy outlined. It became the basic plan for fighting Japan. Marshall was impressed with his knowledge of the situation in Europe and Asia and put him to work preparing America's war plans as Chief of Operations. In fact, he worked so well that in 1942 Marshall promoted him to Major General.[2]

Marshall and Eisenhower agreed that Germany was the main foe and that the United States should focus on the European war. By this time Germany occupied or had troops in a large part of Europe. It even controlled parts of North Africa. After many long discussions with the British, our main ally in the war, it was agreed that a combined force of American and British armies should attack the Germans in North Africa. Eisenhower prepared the plans for the campaign there. It was known as

Operation Torch. Marshall put Eisenhower in command of Torch. Eisenhower was surprised to be made the commander, but he was delighted because he would finally command fighting troops. He liked dealing directly with the fighting soldiers.

The landing of Allied troops in North Africa started in November 1942. It provided Eisenhower with one of his greatest challenges of the war—and one of the most controversial decisions of his career. The French forces in Algiers, a country in North Africa, were under the command of the French Vichy government. It had been formed after Germany defeated France in June 1940. The Vichy government was pro-German and shared some of the ideological and political views of the German ruling party, the Nazis. Not all Frenchmen accepted the Vichy government. Some, known as the Resistance, fought the Germans with guerrilla warfare.

Admiral Jean Darlan commanded the Vichy forces stationed in North Africa. They fought the Americans and British when Operation Torch started. Eisenhower persuaded Darlan to surrender, but only after he agreed that Darlan would remain in control of the French civil government in Algiers. Many people objected to any agreement with a Nazi collaborator. It meant that Jews and Vichy's other political prisoners would remain in Algerian jails. Eisenhower received severe criticism for his "Darlan deal"—a "firestorm of protest," according to one historian.[3]

For Eisenhower, the "Darlan deal" was solely a

military decision. General Marshall supported the decision and estimated that Eisenhower saved approximately sixteen thousand lives.[4] It was, however, a poor political decision. It weakened the morale of the French Resistance, and it probably increased the suspicion of the Soviet Union, the Communist government in Russia and our ally in the war, toward the United States.[5]

Fighting the Germans in Africa was not easy. They were led by General Field Marshal Erwin Rommel, a very capable officer. Only after sending large numbers of reinforcements were the Allies able to defeat him. From there they attacked the island of Sicily in the Mediterranean and then invaded Italy. In Sicily the resistance was strong, but in Italy it was weaker. The Italians were demoralized, and many of them did not like their Fascist leader, Benito Mussolini. Fascists such as Mussolini were dictatorial and violated human rights. They used military power to overcome smaller countries. The anti-Fascist Italians killed Mussolini when the Allies landed. The German leader, Adolf Hitler, quickly reinforced Italy with German troops who fought very well. The fighting in Italy bogged down. Throughout this stage of the war Eisenhower provided firm leadership. He was now preparing to launch the main attack against Germany through France.

As the Allies prepared for the invasion of France, President Roosevelt named Eisenhower the Supreme Allied Commander of the forces in Europe in December

1943. It was now his responsibility to plan, organize, and carry out the destruction of German forces. The toughest part of his job was holding the Allied command together. He frequently argued with British prime minister Winston Churchill and the British commander General Bernard Montgomery over military strategy. On many occasions it was Eisenhower who soothed the easily injured feelings of various generals and politicians. He could be stubborn, but he was best known for being diplomatic and patient. For this he was greatly admired and highly regarded as an excellent commander in both the United States and in Great Britain. He was also popular with the fighting soldiers. He took an interest in their food and treatment in the Army. Newspaper reporters liked his easy manner—and his grin. Eisenhower was now commonly known throughout the world as Ike.[6]

The Allies had to drive the Nazis out of France before the Eisenhower forces could invade Germany. The invasion of France started with the greatest battle of World War II for the United States—D-day, the famous landing of troops on the Normandy coast of France. June 6, 1944, is now recognized as a special day in American history. It was one of several fierce battles that eventually ended the war in Europe.[7]

The Soviets were also fighting the Germans on the eastern front in Europe. That part of the war had started in June 1941, before Germany declared war on the United States. With the invasion of France at Normandy, the Allies were closing in on the Germans on two fronts. On the western front, Eisenhower's area of responsibility, the armies were moving swiftly ahead.

Once he became Supreme Allied Commander, Eisenhower was stationed in headquarters in London. He stayed there for the duration of the war, except when he visited the battlefields. Mamie lived in an apartment in Washington, D.C. Their son, John, attended West

Eisenhower and Prime Minister Winston Churchill of Great Britain during World War II.

Eisenhower eating Army C rations while inspecting the front in North Africa, 1943.

Point. Like other husbands and wives separated by the war, the Eisenhowers missed each other. She sent him small items such as socks and toothbrushes. Knowing her husband liked to read paperback Western novels for relaxation, Mamie sent as many as possible.[8]

Eisenhower wrote over three hundred letters to Mamie during the war. In a letter shortly after the D-day battle, he wrote: "I depend on you and need you. So when you're lonely, try to remember that I'd rather be by your side than anywhere else in the world."[9]

One of the severest tests of both American leadership and the spirit of American soldiers came at the Battle of the Bulge, which took place in Belgium and Luxembourg in December 1944. The Germans launched a surprise counterattack and pushed the Americans back. They almost broke through the American lines. It was a serious situation, and the Allied high command were worried. Some of the Germans dressed as Americans. On one occasion, some Germans massacred over one hundred American prisoners for no reason. When the American troops heard about it, they were furious. They became ferocious fighters and turned the battle around. Eisenhower later wrote that the Battle of the Bulge "became a soldiers' war, [of] sheer courage, and the instinct for survival."[10]

After this point, German resistance seemed to weaken, although Hitler's armies continued to fight hard. In the meantime, the Soviets were advancing against them from the eastern side. Finally, the two armies, Soviet and American, met in April 1945. Various groups of German armies started surrendering. On May 7, 1945, Germany officially surrendered. The war in Europe was over.

Meanwhile, Allied troops were winning victory after victory in the Pacific. This was mainly due to General Douglas MacArthur's leadership, as well as carefully planned attacks. Despite Allied successes, however,

Japan would still not give up. The United States then dropped the atomic bomb for the first time in history. After the Japanese cities of Hiroshima and Nagasaki were completely destroyed, the Axis power finally surrendered. The deadliest war in history officially ended on September 2, 1945.

Eisenhower emerged from the war a world hero. Earlier he had been promoted to Five-Star General, the

Eisenhower (center) at the ruins of Batogne, France, with Generals Omar Bradley (left) and George Patton (right) in 1944.

highest rank in the Army. In Europe and especially the United States he was regarded as the man who held together the Allied war effort and led the crusade for freedom. Even before the Nazis surrendered, German children waved to him in his command car and shouted, "Heil Ice-en-hower."[11] He now received many expressions of gratitude. One of the most impressive was the ticker-tape parade New York City honored him with when he came home. One of the most enjoyable was a parade for him in Abilene. People from all walks of life loved and admired Dwight Eisenhower.[12]

He and Mamie now gave serious thought to retiring, even though he was only fifty-five years old. He considered teaching at a small college, but Eisenhower could not entertain these thoughts for long. In late 1945, the new president, Harry S. Truman, asked him to be Army Chief of Staff, the position held by George Marshall during the war. For the former Allied commander, it was another call to duty that he did not refuse. This job was not as glamorous as leading troops in the war, but he found himself in a familiar position.[13]

Earlier in his career he had worked in Marshall's office, and now he was the Chief of Staff. He had to oversee the demobilization of the armed forces. Eisenhower recognized, of course, the need for reducing military forces, but he did not want American military power to become weak. As Army Chief of Staff he worked closely with President Truman and members of his administration. Frequently he testified before

Dwight D. Eisenhower

SOURCE DOCUMENT

RETURN THIS COPY TO LT.COL. LEE, ADC
ORIGINATORS FILE No. ....

SHAEF MESSAGE FORM

CALL	CIRCUIT No.	PRIORITY	TRANSMISSION INSTRUCTIONS
	NR 2-1		

SPACES WITHIN HEAVY LINES FOR SIGNALS USE ONLY

FROM (A)	ORIGINATOR		DATE-TIME OF ORIGIN
SHAEF FWD	Supreme Commander	DDE/nmr	19 April 1945

TO FOR ACTION   AGWAR

TO (W) FOR INFORMATION (INFO)   EYES ONLY   MESSAGE INSTRUCTIONS GR / 56

(REF NO.)___F W D 1 9 4 6 1___   (CLASSIFICATION)___SECRET EYES ONLY___

WE CONTINUE TO UNCOVER GERMAN CONCENTRATION CAMPS FOR POLITICAL PRISONERS IN WHICH
CONDITIONS OF INDESCRIBABLE HORROR PREVAIL. FROM EISENHOWER TO GENERAL MARSHALL
FOR EYES ONLY.   I HAVE VISITED ONE OF THESE MYSELF AND I ASSURE YOU THAT WHATEVER
HAS BEEN PRINTED ON THEM TO DATE HAS BEEN UNDERSTATEMENT. · IF YOU WOULD SEE ANY
ADVANTAGE IN ASKING ABOUT A DOZEN LEADERS OF CONGRESS AND A DOZEN PROMINENT EDITORS
TO MAKE A SHORT VISIT TO THIS THEATER IN A COUPLE OF C-54s, I WILL ARRANGE TO HAVE
THEM CONDUCTED TO ONE OF THESE PLACES WHERE THE EVIDENCE OF BESTIALITY AND CRUELTY
IS SO OVERPOWERING AS TO LEAVE NO DOUBT IN THEIR MINDS ABOUT THE NORMAL PRACTICES
OF THE GERMANS IN THESE CAMPS.   I AM HOPEFUL THAT SOME BRITISH INDIVIDUALS IN
SIMILAR CATEGORIES WILL VISIT THE NORTHERN AREA TO WITNESS SIMILAR EVIDENCE OF
ATROCITY.

EYES ONLY

DISTRIBUTION :	COORDINATED WITH :		THI or TOR	Opr.
C/S	THIS MESSAGE MUST BE SENT IN CYPHER IF LIABLE TO INTERCEPTION	Precedence / URGENT / ORIGINATING-DIVISION / SHSC		
DOD DIR. 5200.10 DECLASSIFIED NE by W6L date 7-5-67 June 29 1960	INITIALS	NAME AND RANK TYPED. TEL. NO.	TIME CLEARED	
	THIS MESSAGE MAY BE SENT IN CLEAR BY ANY MEANS	Lt.Col.E.R.Lee,ADC 4170		
	INITIALS	AUTHENTICATING SIGNATURE		

General Eisenhower's message to Chief of Staff George Marshall, April 19, 1945. He had just seen the German concentration camps and was horrified. He wanted other leaders to see them.

congressional committees. While he was chief, his son John married Barbara Thompson, and his first grandchild was born in 1948. Eisenhower loved family, home life, and outdoor cookouts. He still liked to grill steaks and hamburgers.[14] While he was chief he started a new hobby, oil painting.

It was during this period, 1945–1948, that the Cold War developed between the United States and the Soviet Union. Although they had been allies in World War II, their suspicion toward each other led to hostility and eventually the Cold War. This term refers to the sharp conflict in diplomacy, trade, and ideology—without actual warfare—that existed between the United States and the Soviet Union.

At the root of their differences was the ideology. The Soviet Union was a Communist nation dedicated to spreading its theories around the world. The United States is a capitalist nation dedicated to defending capitalism and defending other countries from Communist intrusion. Even though the two powers never fought each other militarily, there was always the danger of war breaking out.[15]

At the end of World War II, Eisenhower was friendly toward the Soviets. He had met Soviet General Grigori Zhukov. They admired and respected each other. Eisenhower had also met Soviet leader Joseph Stalin that year and liked him. He even thought the United States and the Soviet Union could be friends.[16] But as strong differences erupted between the two countries,

Eisenhower's attitude toward the Soviet Union changed. One of the most serious concerns of the United States was the Soviet treatment of Eastern European countries. After the war, the Soviet Union continued to occupy some of those countries that it had overrun in fighting the Germans. By mid-1947, Eisenhower no longer trusted the Soviets. He wrote: "Russia is definitely out to communize the world. . . ."[17]

Eisenhower was so popular in the United States that many people wanted him to run for president. In 1948 leaders of both the Democratic and Republican parties asked him to run as their candidate for president. At the Democratic National Convention that year, some leaders of the party started a campaign to get him nominated.[18] He was not interested in politics and refused the invitations. His term as Chief of Staff was for three years, and he was due to be replaced by General Omar Bradley. Bradley had served with him in the war. Again Eisenhower gave serious thought to retiring. He wrote *Crusade in Europe*, his history of World War II in Europe. It sold over a million copies. The book made him and Mamie economically comfortable for the first time since their marriage in 1916.

In 1948, Columbia University asked him to be its president, and he accepted. For the first time since he went to West Point in 1911, he was not fully serving the Army. Working at the university was a new experience for Eisenhower. He liked to be with the students, just as he had enjoyed being with his troops. He stabilized the budget of the school and tried to improve opportunities for the faculty. Even though the job was not as challenging as his other experiences, he found many aspects of it enjoyable. In 1950, while at Columbia, he and Mamie bought a farm at Gettysburg, Pennsylvania, and made plans to remodel it. Mamie designed the remodeling herself.[19]

President Truman asked Eisenhower to serve as an advisor to Secretary of Defense James Forrestal. Eisenhower's rank as a five-star general had put him on "active duty for life."[20] He would not refuse the call to

The inauguration of Eisenhower as president of Columbia University, New York City, in 1948. Mamie watches her husband. Their son, John, in uniform, is seated next to her.

duty, so again he became active in the military affairs of the nation. He combined his job as university president with this new duty. He had to travel a lot between New York and Washington, D.C. He had to work hard to keep up, but he accepted hard work.

Because General Eisenhower was considered an expert on international military affairs, he received many requests to make speeches. He was frequently interviewed by newspaper reporters, and when he spoke, people listened. In 1948 he was ranked in a poll as the first choice for president.[21]

Eisenhower's service to the United States continued. In October 1950, President Truman asked him to serve as commander of the North Atlantic Treaty Organization (NATO). It was a military alliance of the countries of Western Europe, such as Great Britain, France, and Belgium. It included Canada and the United States. It was organized in order to keep the Soviet Union from overrunning Western Europe. A real fear of war with the Soviet Union existed, especially since the Korean War started that year. In January 1951, he and Mamie returned to Europe. Again he was commander of a large international force.

Eisenhower welcomed the NATO command. He was a strong believer in alliances and international cooperation. To withstand pressure from Communist countries, known as the Communist bloc, Eisenhower thought Western nations had to unite both militarily and economically. The United States, he believed, must

Eisenhower, commander of the North Atlantic Treaty Organization (NATO), reports to the nation on television in 1951.

participate and even lead the other NATO countries in the stand against communism. In his diary, he wrote, "I'd like to see the United States able to sit at home and ignore the rest of the world. What a pleasing prospect," he continued, "until you look at the ultimate consequences, destruction."[22]

While he was commanding NATO in 1952, he received more requests to run for president later that year. Even President Truman offered to help him secure the Democratic nomination. Republicans also urged him to run on behalf of their party. All of these requests irritated Eisenhower. Before he went to Europe, he told his friend, Ed Clark, that he could not "even conceive of circumstances as of this moment that would convince me I had a duty to enter politics."[23]

With the election approaching in the fall, however, the pressure on Eisenhower increased. He told some close friends that he was willing to serve as a matter of duty. His new attitude arose from his concern over the isolationist beliefs of some political leaders, especially those of Senator Robert A. Taft of Ohio. Taft was the leading contender for the Republican nomination in 1952. Eisenhower believed the United States should take a leadership role in world affairs. He also wanted a president who would slow the growth of federal domestic programs, which he attributed to the Democrats. Like many career military officers, Eisenhower never publicly revealed his party affiliation. So when he indicated he was a Republican in early 1952, the pressure from this party intensified.[24]

His commitment to run came in February 1952 when he saw a film of a rally for him in New York City. He and Mamie "were profoundly moved," so much so that Eisenhower cried.[25] Eisenhower now knew the public genuinely wanted him. He contacted his friends and Republican supporters and indicated that he was entering the race. His views on America's global responsibilities and domestic issues made him feel a sense of duty to be the next president. He officially announced his candidacy in his hometown of Abilene, Kansas, in June 1952.

His only serious opponent in the Republican party was Senator Taft. Taft almost had the nomination won. Only after some maneuvering by his political managers did Eisenhower receive the nomination. His running mate was Senator Richard M. Nixon of California. The Democrats nominated Governor Adlai Stevenson of Illinois for president.

Eisenhower's campaign went smoothly, although there were some flaws. The most serious was his refusal to criticize Senator Joseph McCarthy of Wisconsin who had earlier insinuated that George Marshall was disloyal.[26] Eisenhower's popularity and sense of command were too much for Stevenson. Eisenhower easily won the election in November 1952. Eisenhower even carried five of the Southern states. Back then the Democratic candidate usually won the election in the Southern states.[27]

The energetic boy from Abilene who used to sell tamales had become president of the United States. He had already had a full career and was famous. It seemed that everything up to this point had prepared him to be president. Now he was embarking on that great task.

5

THE MIDDLE WAY

D wight Eisenhower was the first Republican since Herbert Hoover in the early 1930s to serve as president. When Eisenhower was inaugurated in 1953, the Democrats had dominated American politics for twenty years through the terms of Presidents Franklin D. Roosevelt and Harry S. Truman. During that time, the United States had changed a great deal, especially because of the Depression and World War II. The federal government had expanded greatly, creating many new agencies and programs such as social security. The result was a larger federal government that became more involved in the lives of the American people. Earlier, the Republicans had opposed many of these new programs, and people wondered if Eisenhower would try to destroy them, since he was the first Republican to be elected president for so many years.

Eisenhower did not want to promote the growth of government, but he also did not want to destroy programs such as social security. He referred to his position as the "middle way."[1] The new president felt that "private and local institutions" should be allowed to handle as many problems as possible, but whenever that was impossible, the government should take over.[2] He also wanted to cut federal spending, balance the federal budget, and keep inflation in check. Eisenhower strongly believed that the United States would enjoy prosperity if it followed that course. His view was unpopular with Democrats, who wanted to keep expanding the government. Some Republicans disliked his position because they wanted him to reduce the size and activity of the government. Despite pressure from both sides, Eisenhower stuck with his position, so that during his presidency he supported government action in some respects and opposed it in others.[3]

One example of his support for government action was in the area of health and welfare. In 1953 he persuaded Congress to create the Department of Health, Education and Welfare (HEW). It put the various social programs of the government, scattered among several agencies, into one central agency, HEW. He appointed a woman, Oveta Culp Hobby of Texas, to head the new agency. She was only the second woman ever to be appointed to a Cabinet post.

While Eisenhower was president, HEW fought for increases in social security coverage and federal aid for the construction of hospitals. It distributed the new Salk polio vaccine to the general public. It was the Salk vaccine that ended the scourge of polio, a disease that struck thousands of Americans, particularly children. In 1954 the president urged Congress to pass his Health Reinsurance bill, an example of his "middle way." The proposal would have enabled more Americans to have private health insurance and still keep government out of the health-care industry. Congress refused to pass the bill. Their decision frustrated Eisenhower. Too many members thought the bill would endanger the private practice of doctors. "This plan of ours," he told Republican Senator William Knowland of California, "would have shown the people how we could improve their health and stay out of socialized medicine."[4]

Eisenhower's position toward subsidized agriculture furnishes another example of his "middle way." In 1933, following the leadership of President Franklin D. Roosevelt, the federal government established a program to alleviate the poverty on American farms. Through the program, farmers raised fewer crops and received payment from the government to offset their lost income. The goal was to reduce the agricultural surplus and thereby raise farm prices. By 1953 the program had been modified, but it was still in practice. Paying farmers not to raise crops had always been controversial. Some people wanted it stopped, but it was always justified as a means of aiding farmers.

Ideally, the president wanted farmers to be independent of government support. He appointed Ezra Taft Benson as secretary of agriculture. Benson also wanted to end payments to farmers. But Eisenhower recognized the need to support farmers until they could be self-sustaining. He supported the continued use of payments to farmers, although he usually wanted them to be lower than the farmers liked. The Democrats nearly always wanted to make the payments higher.[5]

His best-known program for agriculture was the soil bank, set up in 1956. It stressed conservation of the soil, but it maintained the payment plan for farmers. Eisenhower thought it was essential to "protect the soil of America just as we want to protect our freedom of speech, right to worship, etc."[6] Although Eisenhower fought the Democrats who wanted to provide greater benefits for farmers, the soil bank program left intact the practice of paying farmers to raise fewer crops.

Generally, Eisenhower opposed public works. He vetoed measures for large-scale public housing and a proposal for economic assistance to depressed areas, known as area redevelopment. He was also against some water development projects such as the McClellan-Kerr Waterway on the Arkansas River in the southwest. He supported the St. Lawrence Seaway, however, that linked the Great Lakes to the Atlantic Ocean. With his prodding, and some pressure from

Canada, Congress approved the construction of the seaway. He ended the Reconstruction Finance Corporation, an old government lending agency dating back to the early Depression years.[7]

One of his most famous projects was the interstate highway system. As more and more people drove cars, the nation's road system badly needed expanding. Eisenhower appreciated the importance of having national highways because of his experience with the Army's cross-country truck convoy in 1919. He assigned his Army colleague, General Lucius D. Clay, to conduct a study of America's congested highways and make recommendations for congressional legislation. In 1956, thanks in great part to Eisenhower's urging, Congress passed the Federal Aid Highway Act. It authorized a forty-one thousand mile system of modern highways. This action started the massive, and popular, interstate highway program.[8]

In 1953, the most pressing problem facing the United States was the Korean War. Previously held by the Japanese, in 1945 Korea was divided into two sectors at the thirty-eighth parallel of north latitude. The Soviet Union, an ally of the United States in World War II, had taken control of the northern half, while the United Nations took the other half. The United Nations was created in 1945 to serve as an organization to resolve international disputes. Under Soviet occupation, North Korea became Communist. South Korea, on the other hand, became more democratic. The United

States played a large role in developing the fledgling South Korean government. Both the Soviets and Americans had left Korea in 1949. Each of the remaining governments, the Republic of Korea in the south and the People's Democratic Republic of Korea in the north, claimed to be the rightful government of all Korea.

The war had started in June 1950 when North Korea invaded South Korea. President Truman had committed the United States to fight the war in order to prevent the spread of communism in Asia. Eisenhower had supported Truman in his decision.[9] Early in the war, after rallying against the surprise invasion, the United States made steady progress, driving deep into North Korea. The military condition worsened, however, and almost became a disaster when the Chinese entered the war in October 1950 on the side of North Korea. The Chinese pushed the United States back to about the thirty-eighth parallel, an imaginary line that cuts Korea approximately in half. The war reached a stalemate, meaning that neither side could make progress. Over twenty thousand soldiers had been killed or were missing when Eisenhower was elected in November 1952. During the campaign Eisenhower promised to visit Korea to make a personal inspection of the military situation there.

Before he was inaugurated as president in November 1952, Eisenhower fulfilled his promise and traveled to Korea. Americans were glad to know he was taking the trip. They trusted him to understand the condition of the war there. He found the Chinese and North Koreans firmly entrenched. He did not think it would be wise to continue fighting there because it would take a much greater effort than was thought to overpower the Communists. He decided to end the war through negotiations.

President Truman had already started negotiations with the North Koreans and Chinese but had not been able to reach an agreement with them. The new president took over the negotiations. He realized he would have to pressure the enemy to get them to agree to end the fighting.

During his inspection of Korea in 1952, Eisenhower (left) eats chow with soldiers of the 3rd Infantry Division.

Eisenhower let the North Koreans and Chinese know that he was willing to make limited use of small atomic weapons. Atomic, or nuclear, weapons, the most deadly in history, had been developed by the United States during World War II. It had used two atomic bombs against Japan in 1945. One bomb destroyed a whole Japanese city—Hiroshima. The American use of those bombs started the Nuclear Age. Small atomic weapons destroyed smaller areas and were meant to be used against enemy soldiers and not civilians. Eisenhower preferred to return to the conditions that existed in Korea before the war started, meaning that the country would be left divided along the thirty-eighth parallel. Once the Communists knew his position about small atomic weapons, Eisenhower wrote that "the prospects for armistice negotiations seemed to improve."[10]

The fighting continued, however, and more Americans were killed. Eisenhower had to cope with the ruler of South Korea, Syngman Rhee, who opposed a peaceful settlement. Rhee wanted to start another push through North Korea. Rhee agreed to accept a settlement only after Eisenhower threatened to withdraw all American forces from Korea. He also promised American aid to Rhee if he would agree. Rhee accepted. Eisenhower never used atomic weapons in the fighting. He continued negotiating with the Communists. Finally, the North Koreans and the Chinese agreed to stop the fighting and signed an armistice on July 27, 1953. The

Korean War was over. Eisenhower was credited with ending an unpopular war.

One of the most difficult problems for Eisenhower was McCarthyism—the anti-Communist hysteria that swept the country during 1950–1954. Historians often point to February 1950 as the beginning of McCarthyism. At that time, Wisconsin Senator Joseph McCarthy made a speech in Virginia in which he claimed to have a list of 205 names of Communists in the United States State Department. If that charge were true, it would have been a serious situation. It would have meant the Soviet Union was obtaining American secrets. But Senator McCarthy never did prove that any such Communists were in the State Department. McCarthyism became a term for the practice of accusing innocent people of being Communists or sympathizing with them. Some people lost their jobs or standing in the community because of false accusations.

Eisenhower detested Senator McCarthy. President Truman and many other people had not liked him either. But McCarthy was chairman of the Senate Subcommittee on Investigation and acted independently of the president. McCarthy had many people who believed in him, including some members of the Senate. His popularity increased because of the widespread fear of communism and the efforts by Communist countries such as the Soviet Union to destroy the American government.[11]

The famous case of the Rosenbergs occurred at this

time. Ethel and Julius Rosenberg were convicted of spying for the Soviet Union. They were convicted of giving away atomic bomb secrets to the Soviets and were executed, although the case was highly controversial. The surprise invasion of South Korea by a Communist government had also increased the fear of communism. Eisenhower later wrote: "McCarthyism was a much larger issue than McCarthy."[12]

Eisenhower did not like Communists either, but he knew that McCarthy was making false accusations and ruining people's lives. Some of the president's advisors wanted him to attack McCarthy publicly, by making a strong speech denouncing him. Eisenhower refused, saying it would be best to ignore him. For the first year of Eisenhower's presidency, therefore, McCarthy continued to hold hearings and accuse people while Eisenhower appeared to be ignoring the situation. Only once did he openly defy McCarthy. Using his executive privilege as president, he refused to let McCarthy have some records of Army personnel. This was an unusual move because in the past, presidents had not withheld information that was subpoenaed, or requested under court order, by Congress. The president continued to ignore McCarthy. He was convinced McCarthy would destroy himself if left alone. "Nothing will be so effective in combatting his particular kind of troublemaking," Eisenhower wrote, "as to ignore him."[13]

In 1954, McCarthy accused U. S. Army officers of helping Communists. This deeply angered Eisenhower

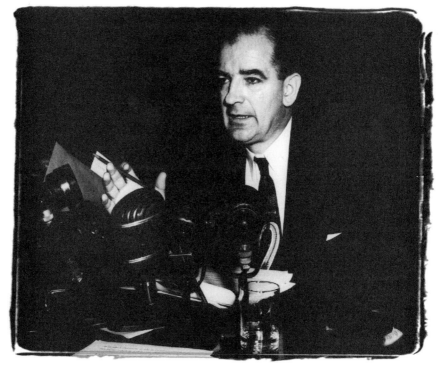

Republican Senator Joseph McCarthy of Wisconsin testified before the Senate Foreign Relations Committee in 1950.

who, of course, was a career Army officer. Behind the scenes, Eisenhower urged that McCarthy's hearings be televised. He wanted the public to see McCarthy in action. He also ordered the Army to find evidence of any wrongdoing by McCarthy or his staff. They discovered that McCarthy had requested the Army to give special favors to one of his staff members who been drafted into the Army.

The discovery of this action hurt McCarthy. As people watched him on television, they grew weary of his accusations. He never produced any proof of his accusations. On television McCarthy appeared gruff and rude. The anti-Communist hysteria was subsiding, due, in part, to the end of the Korean War. McCarthy had received much publicity in the media with his charges, and now the media chose to ignore him. Suddenly McCarthy lost his popular following. He fell into disrepute, and the Senate censured, or publicly disapproved of him in December 1954. He lost his position as chairman of the Investigating Committee. McCarthyism was finally over.[14]

During Eisenhower's presidency the United States enjoyed prosperity, especially during his first term. The American people had many new jobs and increased pay. Family incomes went up. The head of one labor union said: "American labor never had it so good."[15] Usually when incomes rise so well, prices increase, a process known as inflation, which takes away the advantage of better pay. Inflation went up very slowly, meaning the United States enjoyed solid prosperity.

Americans started buying new cars at a record level. They also bought new homes and consumer products such as refrigerators and washing machines. Many people bought their first television set at this time—and more people started going to college. Eisenhower believed that his efforts at cutting government spending were largely responsible for the prosperity. He wanted to balance the budget and keep government activity low, except when the economy needed help.[16]

The combination of peace and prosperity made him

popular. With his well-known grin and easy manner on television, Eisenhower was one of the most admired presidents of the twentieth century. He continued to be known as Ike. Reporters liked to take pictures of him grilling hamburgers or trout-fishing in the Rocky Mountains of Colorado. They took photographs of his grandchildren riding their tricycles inside the White House. Eisenhower's relaxed manner came easily. He projected an image of command and assurance on television, although ironically he sometimes seemed awkward.[17] Television helped him to maintain an excellent relationship with the American people.

Eisenhower often had to host world diplomats and important people at state dinners and banquets at the White House. One of the best known was Queen Elizabeth II of England. Such visits were special occasions that often featured entertainment by popular movie stars or performers like Marion Anderson and Arthur Rubinstein. The Fred Waring Orchestra, popular in the 1950s, appeared more than once. Mamie, as the first lady, always assisted her husband at these state dinners. The White House staff took care of the arrangements, and Mamie made the guests feel comfortable and entertained them as hostess. Her graciousness was a critical part of these functions.

Eisenhower never lost his well-known personal touch with people. Usually at the end of each workday, he liked to spend about an hour chatting with a friend or two in order to relax. He usually stopped work at

6:00 P.M. and looked forward to these moments. The president often invited special friends for dinner. These were not official functions but private dinners, and the guests played cards with him and Mamie. He and Mamie held a Christmas party each year for the White House staff, about eight hundred people.[18]

Dwight and Mamie Eisenhower at the White House.

For relaxation, Eisenhower played golf. His favorite course was at Augusta, Georgia, where the Masters Tournament is held each year. He often arranged for his son, John, and his family to meet him and Mamie there. Golf was Eisenhower's favorite game. He had a putting green installed on the White House lawn so that he could practice. When squirrels started digging holes in the green, the president ordered the pests to be removed and released in a park.[19]

In 1955 Eisenhower had a heart attack while he was visiting Mamie's family in Denver. It created a lot of concern in the government. He stayed in the Fitzsimmons Army Hospital for several weeks but continued to handle his presidential duties. Mamie stayed in a room next to his in order to be close. Vice-President Richard Nixon was prepared to take over if Eisenhower's condition worsened. With the help of aides, the president proved to be capable of taking care of business. He fully recovered from the attack.[20]

Eisenhower enjoyed much success as president. He had ended the Korean War in 1953, a feat he considered his most important accomplishment. The economy was strong and the American standard of living was improving. The public gave him credit for the current peace and prosperity. He seemed to promote unity and served as a symbol of "national consensus."[21] But he always lived with a serious challenge—waging the Cold War against communism.

6

THE COLD WAR: ATOMIC ATTACK?

D uring Eisenhower's first term, the United States fought communism around the world. The former Soviet Union was the world's leader of communism. It was a superpower like the United States and capable of destroying other countries with nuclear weapons. Eisenhower, like all presidents since World War II, wanted to contain communism but avoid war. He dealt with several international crises that could have involved the United States in a general war and in some cases a nuclear war. People worried that the United States always stood in danger of a surprise attack like the one at Pearl Harbor.

When Eisenhower became president, the danger of nuclear war seemed greater than ever. In 1949, the Soviet Union had exploded its first atomic bomb. Then

75

the Americans and Soviets raced to develop hydrogen bombs that were larger and more powerful than previous atomic weapons. The United States exploded one in 1952, and the Soviet Union exploded its first hydrogen bomb the next year. Eisenhower worried that such weapons endangered the world, and wanted to keep them under control.

To demonstrate that he was serious about the possibility of war, he established Operation Outpost Mission, which in case of attack would evacuate the president, his Cabinet, members of Congress, and the Supreme Court to safety outside Washington, D.C. The general public practiced air-raid drills, especially in schools. To prepare for a nuclear attack, students commonly held drills during which they got under their desks. Some people had underground bomb shelters installed in their backyards.[1]

The first crisis that raised the possibility of nuclear war dealt with Formosa, now called Taiwan. Formosa was part of a group of islands off the coast of China. According to Eisenhower, the Formosan crisis could "seemingly carry the country to the edge of war."[2] In China the Nationalists had been in charge of the Chinese government and were supported by the United States. In 1949, the Chinese Communists, under the leadership of Chairman Mao Tse-tung, won control of China. The Communists forced the Chinese Nationalist forces, led by Chiang Kai-shek, onto the islands of Formosa, and the smaller islands of Quemoy and Matsu. A large number of Nationalist troops occupied the latter two islands, but they were no match for the huge forces of Communist China. Chairman Mao vowed to drive the Nationalists off the islands.

In September 1954 the Chinese started shelling Quemoy and Matsu with artillery. These islands were close to China but were not strategically important. They had, however, much symbolic value. Eisenhower decided they should be protected, but he did not think they were worth a war with China.

He received much advice on the matter. Some of his advisors wanted him to establish a blockade of China or order air strikes against it. There were others who wanted him to abandon Quemoy and Matsu.[3] Nearly all the suggestions required speedy action on his part. Eisenhower knew he had to avoid war and resisted the pleas for fast action. The United States also had to worry about the Soviet Union which could intervene on behalf of the Chinese Communists. If it did not intervene, the Soviet Union might still provide weapons and supplies to them. "If we get into a general war," the president told his advisors, "the logical enemy will be Russia, not China, and we will have to strike there."[4]

First he obtained a statement of support from Congress. Then he let China know that the United States would firmly defend Formosa. Eisenhower decided to defend Quemoy and Matsu only if the Chinese used them to invade Formosa. He wanted to exercise patience: "The hard way," he said, "is to have the courage to be patient."[5]

Eisenhower let the world know of his determination to defend Formosa, and he hinted at using small atomic weapons. Secretary of State John Foster Dulles persuaded the Soviet Union to ask China to stop harassing the Nationalists. Soon the Chinese indicated they wanted no war and stopped shelling Quemoy and Matsu. The crisis was over rather suddenly in May 1955. Eisenhower had prevailed. He kept Formosa free and avoided war.[6]

Another international crisis developed in Asia. It did not directly threaten the United States, but it had long-term consequences. It was the French war with the Vietnamese Communists. The United States did not enter the war while Eisenhower was president. However, some important events occurred there during his first term that help explain the American intervention in the 1960s.

Vietnam is located in Southeast Asia, just south of China. The French had controlled Vietnam before World War II but were driven out by the Japanese in 1940. At the end of the war, the French were back in control, but they were unpopular, and the people of Vietnam started a rebellion against them. The Vietnamese followed the leadership of Ho Chi Minh, who was a Communist. The Communists steadily outfought the French. Then a critical battle occurred at Dien Bien Phu in 1954. Needing military support, the French asked Eisenhower to provide air strikes against the Communists at Dien Bien Phu. At one point they asked for American troops—and wanted them to fight under French command.

Eisenhower refused to send troops into Vietnam. He would not authorize air strikes to help the French. He doubted that air strikes would be effective in the jungle terrain of Vietnam. The president definitely opposed sending troops to fight under French command.[7] He wanted America's allies in Europe such as Great Britain to help, too, but they refused. Eisenhower would not intervene unless the other countries also participated. Another consideration was the strong feeling against the French in Vietnam. Until the Vietnamese people supported the French more, Eisenhower did not want the United States to risk the lives of its soldiers. In 1954 the French lost the battle at Dien Bien Phu, ending the French rule in Vietnam.

The final settlement of the war in Vietnam came with the Geneva Accords. It was an international agreement that separated the country into two zones at the seventeenth parallel.[8] The Communists occupied the northern zone while the anti-Communist forces of Vietnam stayed in the southern zone. Eisenhower was opposed to the growth of communism in Vietnam. With the help of Secretary of State Dulles, he persuaded those countries with an interest in Southeast Asia to form the Southeast Asia Treaty Organization (SEATO). Eisenhower hoped that this alliance, which included Great Britain, France, Australia, and some other countries, would stop the growth of communism in Vietnam. It did not, but it did commit the United States to supporting the non-Communist government which prevailed in South Vietnam.

Toward the end of Eisenhower's first term, an incident exploded in the Middle East. It was the Egyptian seizure of the Suez Canal. The Suez Canal, located in Egypt, is a vital passageway for world trade. It provides a water route for ships, particularly tankers carrying oil from the Middle East, to reach Europe and the United States. Without the Suez Canal, ships would have to travel around the southern tip of Africa. The British had built the canal and finished it in 1869. Many countries of the world used the canal, but Great Britain and France controlled and operated it.[9] These two countries wanted to keep their power and influence in the Middle East.

The crisis began with the rise of a new leader in Egypt, Gamal Nasser. He wanted to assert the authority of his people, the Egyptians, and all Arabs in the Middle East. In July 1956, Nasser "nationalized" or seized control of the canal. That meant Egypt would take over the operation of the passageway so vital to world trade. Nasser felt that since it was in Egypt, his own people should control it. The seizure frightened the British and French. They did not think the Egyptians were capable of operating the canal. Great Britain would also feel a loss of international prestige if Egypt kept the canal.[10] Great Britain and France wanted to invade Egypt and recapture the canal with military force.

Eisenhower opposed the use of military force to resolve the dispute. Egyptians were also moving ships successfully through the canal despite the British lack of faith in their competence. Eisenhower wanted the matter to be worked out peacefully through the United Nations. The United Nations had been set up in 1945. It tried to prevent war by resolving international disputes. Despite the president's position, the British and French planned to use troops.

While Eisenhower tried to resolve the Egyptian seizure of the Suez Canal, an uprising against Communist leadership occurred in Poland. The Soviet Union controlled Poland, but it was unpopular there. This uprising was not successful, and the Soviets remained in control. However, it inspired and encouraged the people of Hungary who also lived unhappily under Soviet rule. In October 1956, they rebelled against the Communist government in their country, starting the Hungarian revolt. This was one of the major rebellions against the Soviets during the Cold War. The Hungarians appealed to the United States for help, but Eisenhower refused to assist them.[11]

Some people at the time thought Eisenhower should send help to the Hungarians, especially since the United States had encouraged people living under communism to fight for their freedom. But Eisenhower did not want to risk war with the Soviet Union. Hungary was one of its satellite countries, and direct involvement with American troops or other support would mean a direct military confrontation between the Americans and the Soviets. Eisenhower had always been cautious about

Citizens of Budapest tear down a statue of Soviet dictator Joseph Stalin during the Hungarian revolt of 1956.

making commitments to help Soviet-controlled countries in Europe.[12]

Hungary presented special problems, too. It was not accessible by sea, so the United States could not use its navy. Hungary was surrounded by other Soviet satellite countries and "sending United States troops alone into Hungary through hostile or neutral territory," Eisenhower wrote, "would have involved us in general war."[13]

Meanwhile the crisis in Egypt worsened. In October 1956, Israel invaded Egypt in the Sinai Peninsula because it thought Nasser's goal of uniting Arabs threatened it. Egypt tried to defend itself from Israel. Great Britain and France issued an ultimatum to Egypt, demanding that it let them come into Egypt with troops in order to protect the Suez Canal. Nasser refused, and when the British bombed some Egyptian targets, Nasser blocked the canal by sinking over thirty ships in it.[14] Eisenhower was determined not to let the fighting in the Middle East involve the United States, and he did not want to let it lead to a major war. Nasser tried to stop Israel but could not. Nasser then tried to keep the British and French away from the canal.

The Hungarians continued their revolt until early November when the Soviets sent over two hundred thousand troops and four thousand tanks into Hungary and crushed the rebellion. At the same time, the Soviets promised to help Nasser against the British and French. Eisenhower warned the Soviets that such a move would be foolish and that he would not allow it. He told one advisor that if Russian troops fought the British and French, "we would, of course, be in a major war."[15] Despite their differences over Suez, the United States and Great Britain remained allied against communism.

Eisenhower wanted to stop the fighting. First, he put the American forces stationed in the Middle East on special alert as a warning to the Soviets. Then, he kept pressure on the British and French to let the United Nations resolve the dispute. On November 6, 1956, Israel stopped fighting and the British announced a cease-fire. Nasser had agreed to allow a peacekeeping force to protect the canal until the questions over it could be resolved. The Soviets sent no troops, and a larger war was avoided. Throughout the crisis, Eisenhower remained calm. "He reinforced his image," wrote one

Republican party campaign literature from the 1956 election. Eisenhower was too busy with the Suez crisis and the Hungarian revolt to spend much time campaigning.

historian, "as the man around whom Americans could rally in the time of crisis."[16]

Both the Suez crisis and Hungarian revolt occurred during the presidential campaign of 1956, so Eisenhower did not have time to make many speeches. He was still very popular though. Large crowds greeted him around the country when he made public appearances. The Republicans reused their campaign slogan of 1952: "I Like Ike." His Democratic opponent was Adlai Stevenson, who ran against him in 1952. Eisenhower won the election easily, getting a larger margin of votes than in 1952.

With the withdrawal of the British and French from Egypt, it was necessary for the United States to provide leadership and assistance in the Middle East. Eisenhower proposed to Congress a program of economic and military aid to the countries there in order to oppose Communist influence. Congress approved his plan and it became known as the Eisenhower Doctrine.[17]

These crises presented a real danger that the United States might get into armed conflict or possibly a nuclear confrontation with the Soviet Union while Eisenhower was president. He wanted to resolve disputes with wise, patient action. On several occasions, to be sure, he pushed the Communists to the edge of war, but he managed to maintain the peace. He knew what he decided could lead to military action, and he used his knowledge of military operations and strategy in making these fateful decisions.

7

KEEPING PEACE IN A TURBULENT WORLD

Preventing war and keeping the United States safe from nuclear attack were not the only difficulties Eisenhower faced. During his second term he had to deal with domestic problems within the United States. He used patience and arranged settlements as often as possible. In 1957, however, he dealt with one of the most serious incidents of his presidency—the crisis resulting from the integration of Little Rock Central High School in Arkansas.

The incident was part of the larger civil rights movement. Eisenhower considered himself to be sympathetic to the cause of civil rights. He had appointed Herbert Brownell, who favored school integration, as the attorney general. Eisenhower was largely responsible for the desegregation of Washington, D.C. He also completed the integration of the military service started by former President Truman. Eisenhower was largely responsible for the 1957 Civil Rights Act passed by Congress. It was the first civil rights federal legislation passed since 1875.[1] In 1954 the Supreme Court ruled that racial segregation was illegal in public schools. Eisenhower was not a segregationist, but he never took a strong position on behalf of integration. He thought many Americans, particularly Southerners, would strongly resist integration. He felt it should proceed through the court system.

The school district in Little Rock planned to integrate its schools in September 1957 by enrolling nine African-American students in Central High School. Many people in the area were opposed to the plan and wanted to prevent the enrollment of the nine students. Arkansas Governor Orval Faubus ordered the state National Guard into Little Rock to maintain law and order. The governor also ordered the Guard not to let the students enroll, claiming they might be hurt. When the students arrived to start school, the Guardsmen turned them away. This action defied the federal court, which had ordered the school district to integrate.[2]

Governor Faubus realized that he had a crisis on his hands because of the large number of people threatening to use violence to keep the African-American students out of Central High. He asked President Eisenhower for a personal conference to discuss the matter. Eisenhower was in Newport, Rhode

Island, for a short vacation and told Faubus to come there for the meeting. At this meeting Eisenhower indicated that he wanted the African-American students enrolled. He asked Faubus to change his orders for the National Guard—to order them to let the students enroll and protect them if necessary.[3]

Faubus did not change the orders. He sent the National Guard home, leaving the local police responsible for keeping law and order at the school. The governor then left for a conference in Georgia. On Monday, September 23, when the nine students were returning to enroll, a mob of one thousand people had gathered at the high school. Some violence erupted. Again the students were sent home. The next day the mob was back and the mayor of Little Rock, Woodrow Wilson Mann, asked Eisenhower to send troops in order to control the mob.

Eisenhower did not want to get involved in the incident. He thought he had worked out an arrangement with Faubus. Now he had to enforce the court order. He always thought that enforcing the law and protecting the Constitution was his duty. So despite his hopes of avoiding the incident at Little Rock, he ordered one thousand paratroops into the city with instructions to enroll the African-American students. He also federalized the Arkansas National Guard. It was now under his command and it assisted the paratroopers. As much as he disliked this action, Eisenhower felt it was his duty—a matter of upholding the law. Earlier he had written to his friend Swede Hazlett: "If the day comes when we can obey the orders of our courts only when we personally approve of them, the end of the American system, as we know it, will not be far off."[4]

The troops escorted the African-American students into the school. They drove the protesters away from the building. Some troops rode in military vehicles. It was clearly a use of military force to maintain law and order. Eisenhower did not like using troops against American citizens, but he thought he had to do it.

By November all of the paratroops were gone. The president left a small force of the National Guard there until the end of the school year. There was no more violence. The following year, 1958, Governor Faubus closed the public schools in Little Rock. It was a ploy to avoid integrating the schools there. During that year the white students attended classes set up by the Little Rock Private School Corporation.[5] The schools in the district reopened the next year as public schools only after a federal court ordered them to. In that case, Eisenhower took no action.

Even though Eisenhower used his power as president to ensure the integration of schools in Little Rock, he did not actively push for integration in a broader sense. He believed in protecting the Constitution and upholding the law, but otherwise stayed out of local affairs. The president wanted integration to proceed along legal lines as much as possible but did not push

SOURCE DOCUMENT

RECEIVED
OCT - 2 1957
CENTRAL FILES

Checked by Kardos

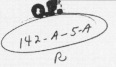
142-A-5-A
R̄

I. JACK MARTIN

NIGHT LETTER

Newport, Rhode Island
September 27, 1957

The Honorable Richard B. Russell
United States Senate
Washington, D. C.

Few times in my life have I felt as saddened as when the
obligations of my office required me to order the use of
force within a state to carry out the decisions of a Federal
Court. My conviction is that had the police powers of the
State of Arkansas been utilized not to frustrate the orders
of the Court but to support them, the ensuing violence and
open disrespect for the law and the Federal Judiciary would
never have occurred. The Arkansas National Guard could
have handled the situation with ease had it been instructed to
do so. As a matter of fact, had the integration of Central
High School been permitted to take place without the intervention of the National Guard, there is little doubt that the
process would have gone along quite as smoothly and quietly
as it has in other Arkansas communities. When a State, by x of 147
seeking to frustrate the orders of a Federal Court, encourages
mobs of extremists to flout the orders of a Federal Court, and
when a State refuses to utilize its police powers to protect against
mobs persons who are peaceably exercising their right under the
Constitution as defined in such Court orders, the oath of office
x of 102-B of the President requires that he take action to give that protection.
Failure to act in such a case would be tantamount to acquiescence
in anarchy and the dissolution of the union.

I must say that I completely fail to comprehend your comparison
of our troops to Hitler's storm troopers. In one case military
power was used to further the ambitions and purposes of a ruthless
dictator; in the other to preserve the institutions of free government.

You allege certain wrong-doings on the part of individual soldiers

- 2 -

at Little Rock. The Secretary of the Army will assemble the
facts and report them directly to you.

With warm regard,

DWIGHT D. EISENHOWER

*Eisenhower defends his use of troops in the Little Rock, Arkansas,
integration incident in a letter to Senator Richard B. Russell,
September 27, 1957.*

the process. Civil rights leaders disagreed with his way of handling the situation.[6] But his action in Little Rock indicated that court orders on integration would definitely be enforced.

The Little Rock incident was not the first crisis to erupt in 1957. In October, Russia launched *Sputnik*, the first man-made space satellite. *Sputnik* was a surprise for the general public. It caused concern over America's leadership in the Cold War. Some commentators regarded the *Sputnik* launch as another Pearl Harbor. Democratic Senator Henry Jackson of Washington wanted the country to proclaim a "week of shame and danger."[7] The *Sputnik* launching was a famous event in world history because it was the first satellite to orbit the earth.

Eisenhower was not surprised by *Sputnik*. His advisors had told him that the Soviets might soon launch a satellite. Now, he had to convince the public that *Sputnik* and the Soviet space program were not a threat. He quickly met with scientific experts who agreed that the satellite did not pose any danger to the United States. Then, Eisenhower held a press conference. He remained calm and confident and assured the public that the country was safe from Soviet attack.[8]

Next, he took steps to improve our space program which was already underway. He ordered the Army and Navy to coordinate their activities in space research. The president asked Congress to establish an educational program to encourage students to pursue careers in science, math, and engineering. In 1958,

Dwight D. Eisenhower

: Telephone
MUrray Hill 2-0500

425 LEXINGTON AVENUE

New York 17, N. Y.

THE WHITE HOUSE

Jun 12 9 33 AM '58

RECEIVED

June 10, 1958

The President
The White House
Washington, D. C.

My dear Mr. President:

I was very pleased at the contents of your letter and extremely
happy about your personal tribute to me. However, my concern isn't for personal achievements but for the accomplishment of our nation and the part 17 million loyal Negro Americans can play in bringing about equality for all Americans.

We have a great stake in our country's development, and we
are in a period where teamwork and cooperation will deter-
mine the progress we continue to make.

It is with this thought in mind, I respectfully request your
giving consideration to having a meeting with Negro leaders
in an effort to further our progress of mutual understanding.
Unfortunately, too many Negro leaders and Negro masses
misinterpret your statement about patience. They consider
that you favor patience alone rather than patience backed up
when necessary with law enforcement.

It is my view that a meeting by you with responsible Negro
leadership in the near future would help clarify and advance
the cause of equal rights for all of our citizens and thus e-
liminate some of the unfavorable propaganda used by our en-
emies abroad.

Respectfully yours,

Jackie Robinson

Jackie Robinson

JR:cc

June 10, 1958: Baseball star Jackie Robinson urges President Eisenhower to meet with African-American leaders and explain his position on civil rights.

President Eisenhower's first press conference, held on October 9, 1957, after Russia launched its satellite Sputnik.

Congress passed the National Defense Education Act. It was widely believed that the United States needed to increase its number of scientists and engineers, or else risk falling further and further behind the Soviets in the field of technical superiority.

The Soviets remained ahead in space research and development. Soon after *Sputnik*, they launched a second satellite, a large one weighing eleven hundred pounds, which carried a small dog named Laika. America's space program was slow. The first American satellite, *Vanguard*, exploded on the launching pad soon after Laika went into space.[9] Although the failure did not endanger the country, it was embarrassing for the United States.

A few months later, progress improved. In January

1958, *Explorer I*, the first American satellite, went into orbit. Soon *Explorer II* and *III* were launched. Next, Congress and Eisenhower, working together, created the National Aeronautical and Space Administration (NASA). They made it responsible for handling the space program. In 1960, NASA started the Mercury project, which put the first American astronauts into space. By the end of Eisenhower's presidency, the United States had launched thirty-one satellites.[10] The famous *Apollo 11* landing on the moon, however, came much later—not until 1969.

In November 1957 Eisenhower suffered a minor stroke. One day, while sitting at his desk, he felt dizzy and noticed he could not pick up a pen. Unable to talk he signaled for his secretary. Doctors were called immediately. They put him to bed. The president improved rapidly and went ahead with plans to attend a NATO meeting scheduled for December. Eisenhower knew the trip would test his ability to perform in public. His performance at NATO was excellent and the meeting was a success. He continued to work well as president, but he noticed thereafter that he sometimes had trouble "finding the word" he wanted and that he occasionally reversed the syllables of long words.

For the rest of his presidency, Eisenhower dealt with one crisis after another in both domestic and foreign affairs. As far back as 1953 he urged Congress to accept Hawaii into the Union. Only after much prodding from Secretary of the Interior Fred Seaton, however, did

Eisenhower recommend statehood for Alaska. Congress admitted Alaska in 1958 and Hawaii in 1959.[11]

The president had no reprieve from international crises. In July 1958 he sent troops to Lebanon. It was the only crisis in which he sent troops overseas. Lebanon is a small country in the Middle East. In 1958 its president, Camille Chamoun, was friendly to the United States. That year serious riots broke out in Lebanon in opposition to Chamoun because his opponents thought he wanted to serve another term as president.[12] According to Lebanese law, he could serve only one term. His opponents were also followers of Egypt's leader, Nasser, who was still on friendly terms with the Soviet Union. There was a natural belief, though perhaps unfounded, that Nasser's pro-Arab

President Eisenhower relaxes with his favorite game, golf, in Newport, Rhode Island, August 1958.

activity, plus his Soviet connections, would eventually mean trouble in the Middle East.

Eisenhower hoped the unrest in Lebanon would not require American intervention, but in July 1958 the president of Iraq was overthrown. At the same time, another country in the Middle East, Jordan, experienced unrest. Eisenhower believed that the whole Middle East was in turmoil. He did not intend to allow Nasser's influence to grow. Nasser, Eisenhower thought, might let the Soviets establish themselves in the area. Such a development, from Eisenhower's point of view, would endanger the oil supply that the United States and other Western nations needed.

In July 1958 he ordered American military forces to occupy Beirut, the capital city of Lebanon. He instructed them not to go beyond the city limits. When the troops landed, they were welcomed by the people in the city. There was no fighting. The Soviet Union strongly objected to the intervention, but Eisenhower never worried about the Soviets fighting a war over Lebanon. The troops stayed there for two months. Both the Lebanese and Iraqis elected new presidents who were friendly to the United States. This settled the situation in Lebanon.

Eisenhower later wrote that fast action was necessary in Lebanon. He did not want to wait for the United Nations. He also wanted to show Nasser, who he thought was behind some of the unrest in the Middle East, that the United States would not let him act unchallenged.[13]

While the troops were in Lebanon, another crisis broke out over Formosa. This was an even more dangerous situation than the first Formosan crisis of 1954. The Chinese Communists again tried to capture the islands of Quemoy and Matsu. They established a "blockade" of the islands by firing artillery shells, as many as eight thousand rounds per day, at the Chinese Nationalist troops there. The Communists hoped to keep the Nationalist government on Formosa from resupplying the troops.

Eisenhower considered this second crisis more dangerous than the first for two reasons. Since 1955, the Soviets had increased their nuclear stronghold, and the Chinese Communists had built new airfields near Quemoy and Matsu. The president still believed the Soviet Union was backing the Chinese, a consideration that increased the risk of nuclear war. After consulting with his advisors, Eisenhower took the same position he had taken in the first crisis.[14]

The United States made clear its determination to defend Formosa. In the meantime it would assist the Nationalists trying to "run" the blockade with supply ships. American ships would, however, be kept away from the shelling. Gradually, the Nationalists learned how to run their ships through the blockade. The Communists realized their effort to starve the Nationalist troops on Quemoy and Matsu was failing. After a while they lost interest in the islands, and the second Formosan crisis was over.

Eisenhower and Mao Tse-tung had played "cat and mouse" with each other over Formosa. Eisenhower, the old poker player, was good at such ploys, maintaining his reputation as a brilliant military strategist. The Communists realized they were dealing with a wise military leader who had the backing of his people. By the same token, Quemoy and Matsu were not important enough to the Chinese for them to risk war.

This victory over communism, however, was ruined by another crisis, one that embarrassed Eisenhower: the *U-2* flight over the Soviet Union in 1960.

As the two superpowers, the United States and the Soviet Union, raced each other for military superiority, they also spied on each other. Spying was part of the Cold War. In July 1955, Eisenhower had proposed that the United States and the Soviet Union have an "Open Skies" agreement. It would let each country send airplanes over the other and take aerial photographs of military and missile bases. The president thought this plan would promote peace. It would also work to the advantage of the United States since it needed to know more about the Soviet Union. The Soviet government rejected the proposal.

Disappointed over the rejection, Eisenhower relied on the flights of a new plane. It was the *U-2*, a reconnaissance, or spy, plane designed to take photographs from more than sixty thousand feet above the ground. The photographs could show details of military and missile bases. In 1956, the president ordered *U-2* flights over the Soviet Union from bases in Europe. The Soviets knew about the flights and protested to the Eisenhower administration about them, but could not stop them. However, the Soviets did not protest the flights publicly, because that would have been an admission that they could not stop them.[15]

By 1960, the Soviets had improved their missiles. They could now launch Intercontinental Ballistic Missiles (ICBMs) with nuclear warheads at the United States. Some of Eisenhower's critics alleged that the United States had a missile gap, meaning the Soviets had more missiles.[16] Eisenhower wanted to know for sure how many missiles they had, so he ordered another *U-2* flight over Russia to take place in May 1960. He wanted it to be the last.

The famous *U-2* flight occurred on May 1, 1960. It was not the first "spy flight" over Russia, but it was the first the Soviets shot down. The pilot, Francis Gary Powers, was captured alive. This was a dangerous situation for the United States because *U-2* flights violated Soviet airspace.

The president, wrote one historian, "tried to conceal the nature of the mission."[17] The United States stated that the *U-2* was a weather plane that strayed into the Soviet Union. The Russians knew better. Eisenhower authorized a second statement, saying it was a NASA plane that drifted over the Soviet Union. The president hoped to cover up the incident. In other words, he did not want to acknowledge the *U-2* flights. Finally, the

In 1960, photographs of U-2 pilot Francis Gary Powers were publicly displayed in Moscow.

Soviet leader, Nikita Khrushchev, announced that the pilot was alive and being held captive.

News reporters and critics now questioned the president's role in the matter. His advisors urged him to keep issuing cover stories. He wanted to tell the truth. He did not want his staff to be blamed for his decision. If he denied his knowledge of the *U-2* flight, it would appear that he was not in control of his job. Eisenhower also thought the integrity of the White House was at stake. "And it would have been untrue," he wrote later, if he had continued to deny his responsibility.[18] The people must be able, he insisted, to believe the president. Finally, he acknowledged his responsibility for the *U-2* flight.

The incident ruined a summit conference of the "Big Four" set for a short time later in Paris. The Big Four consisted of the United States, the Soviet Union, Great Britain, and France. They were known as the Big Four because they were the four largest military powers. The meeting had been scheduled before the disastrous *U-2* flight. At the meeting, Khrushchev demanded an apology from Eisenhower. Eisenhower refused to apologize. He knew the Soviets spied on the United States, although not with *U-2* flights. Khrushchev walked out of the meeting and the summit ended.

The failure of the meeting was a great disappointment for Eisenhower. He wanted to improve relations with the Soviet Union, but now there was a stronger sense of suspicion and hostility between the two countries. He felt the *U-2* incident had ruined his chances for

Dwight D. Eisenhower

SOURCE DOCUMENT

~~TOP SECRET~~

November 24, 1954

MEMORANDUM OF CONFERENCE WITH THE PRESIDENT
0810   24 November 1954

Others present: Secretary of State
                   (for part of meeting)
                   Secretary of Defense
                   Mr. Allen Dulles
                   Secretary of Air Force
                   General Twining
                   Lt. General Cabell
                   Lt. General Putt
                   Colonel Goodpaster

Authorization was sought from the President to go ahead on a program to produce thirty special high performance aircraft at a cost of about $35 million.   The President approved this action.   Mr. Allen Dulles indicated that his organization could not finance this whole sum without drawing attention to it, and it was agreed that Defense would seek to carry a substantial part of the financing.

The Secretary of Defense sought the President's agreement to taking one last look at the type of operations planned when the aircraft are available.   The President indicated agreement.

To a question by the President, the Secretary of State indicated that difficulties might arise out of these operations, but that "we could live through them."

In summary, the President directed those present to go ahead and get the equipment, but before initiating operations to come in for one last look at the plans.

A. J. Goodpaster

 TOP SECRET

Memo issued by President Eisenhower's staff member, A. J. Goodpaster. It shows that in 1954 the president approved a program to build U-2 airplanes to spy on Russia.

"ending the Cold War."[19] Eisenhower had gambled that the last *U-2* flight would not be detected, but he lost.

As his presidency approached its end, he faced another development in the Cold War. This one occurred close to the United States. The ruler of Cuba at that time, Fulgencio Batista, was very unpopular. In 1958 a popular revolt erupted against Batista under the leadership of Fidel Castro. In January 1959, Castro and his forces took over Cuba.[20]

At first Castro seemed friendly toward the United States. But Eisenhower quickly became frustrated with the new Cuban leader. For one thing, Castro ordered the execution of many officers who had fought against him. Also, Castro announced that he would not support the United States in the Cold War and complained about American interference in Cuba. Soon, prominent Communist leaders of the world like Mao Tse-tung of China, praised him. To an extent, Castro's dislike of the United States was related to American support of Batista. Eisenhower was also slow to realize the general resentment toward the United States in Latin America.[21]

Castro established a Communist government in the Western Hemisphere, something the United States had wanted to prevent. Eisenhower did not want Castro to succeed. He arranged for the United States to stop buying sugar from Cuba. He also took a good-will tour of Latin America in order to counter the influence of Castro. Eisenhower received a great welcome, but he was disturbed by evidence of Castro's popularity.

The president instructed the Central Intelligence Agency (CIA) to start training Cuban exiles as a military force to overthrow Castro. The exiles were non-Communists who had fled Castro's government. The training took place in Guatemala. Eisenhower did not make any final plans about the use of the exiles.

By September 1960 the relationship between the United States and Cuba had worsened, and Eisenhower evacuated Americans living there. In January 1961 he cut off official diplomatic relations with Cuba. A few days later, however, America had a new president, John F. Kennedy, and Eisenhower could do no more.[22] His experience with Castro was the beginning of the events that eventually led to the famous Bay of Pigs invasion of Cuba when Kennedy was president. The Bay of Pigs invasion occurred in April 1961. President John F. Kennedy tried to overthrow Castro by using the force of Cuban exiles which had been started by Eisenhower. The invasion failed.

As Eisenhower prepared to leave the White House, he wanted to make a "final address" to the American people.[23] His primary concern was still the security of the United States. He had built up the military forces since becoming president in 1953 primarily because of the Cold War, but he did not want the country to become a "garrison state."[24] In his farewell address, he warned of the danger of spending too much money on defense. The country has other needs, he said, and they should not suffer for the sake of unnecessary military

SOURCE DOCUMENT

Ford, I must express my gratitude to the radio and television networks of the motion picture opportunities they have given me, over the years to bring special messages to our people. My special thanks go to them on this [illegible]

MY FELLOW AMERICANS

THREE DAYS from now,
after half a century in the service
of our country, I shall lay down
the responsibilities of office as,
in traditional and solemn ceremony,
the authority of the Presidency
is vested in my successor.

THIS EVENING I come to you
with a message of leave-taking
and farewell, and to share
a few final thoughts with you,
my countrymen.

The reading copy of Eisenhower's farewell speech, January 17, 1961. He used this copy when he addressed the American people. He had written notes at the top, but scratched them out.

spending. He referred to the "military-industrial complex," the combination of a "military establishment and a large arms industry."[25] He warned that this complex could use its powerful influence and cause the government to spend too much money on defense. This speech became one of his most famous.[26]

When Kennedy took over the White House, Eisenhower retired from public life. For the first time since he had left Abilene in 1911 for West Point, he was not in service to the United States. After Kennedy's inauguration, Ike and Mamie quietly drove to their home in Gettysburg.

President Eisenhower welcomes President-elect John F. Kennedy to the White House, December 6, 1960.

8

RETIREMENT
AND LEGACY

Eisenhower enjoyed retirement. He relaxed and had fun. He and Mamie devoted time to their grandchildren, to their hobbies, and to their farm at Gettysburg. They remained popular, too, with the general public. Americans ranked Eisenhower as "the most admired, respected and popular man in the country" even after he left the White House.[1]

Ike and Mamie kept busy. He would spend half a day in his office at nearby Gettysburg College, working on his memoirs and meeting visitors. On a typical day Eisenhower might walk over his farm, examining his Black Angus cattle. He devoted more time to his painting. Ike and Mamie enjoyed sitting on the front porch together. Their house was large, and Mamie decorated it with the furniture and personal belongings they had acquired since their marriage in 1916. A grand piano sat near the front of the house. Mamie decorated the bedrooms in pink and green. On her dresser she kept a photograph of her husband when he had been a cadet at West Point.[2]

The farm was next to the site of the famous Civil War battle of Gettysburg. Eisenhower enjoyed reviewing and analyzing the battle and took visitors on walking tours of the site. His most famous visitor in this regard was President Charles De Gaulle of France, Eisenhower's old friend from World War II. News photographers took pictures of the two famous generals reliving the Gettysburg battle.

Outdoor cookouts were popular at the farm. Eisenhower still enjoyed grilling for family and friends. He played a lot of golf, his favorite recreational pastime. He had a putting green built close to the house. One day a horse got loose and left its hoofprints on the green. Eisenhower, whose family expected him to explode in rage, remained calm and thought little of it.[3] In 1967 he made a hole-in-one while playing golf in Palm Desert, California. He was thrilled and regarded it as one of the highlights of his life.

Although Eisenhower was no longer in public service, the country still demanded a lot of him. He received requests to endorse fund-raising plans and to be a member of various foundations and institutes. He refused most, helping only those he felt were worthy causes. He supported the new Eisenhower College in

Seneca Falls, New York. And he answered a large volume of mail.[4]

Eisenhower made a great contribution when he wrote a two-volume memoir of his presidency. In it he explained all the major developments and crises of his presidency. He wanted to establish a record of the 1950s from his point of view. He also wrote *At Ease*, probably his most popular book. It was a personal history of his life. In it he recalled his childhood in Abilene, Kansas, and his career in the Army. Indeed, his books were an outstanding achievement.

During his retirement the United States had two presidents: John F. Kennedy and Lyndon B. Johnson. Although they were Democrats, both of them sought Eisenhower's advice. He remained committed to fighting communism and supported both men in that respect. Kennedy decided to go forward with the invasion of Cuba at the Bay of Pigs. Eisenhower was disappointed when the invasion failed. Eisenhower thought Kennedy had mismanaged the invasion.[5] He was not always happy with Kennedy's decisions. He usually did not disagree over the goal, but rather over how to achieve it.

Eisenhower supported President Johnson as well. Johnson consulted him about the Vietnam War. Eisenhower fully agreed that the United States should defend the South Vietnamese from communism. He urged Johnson, however, to use more force. He also urged Johnson to give the American commander in

SOURCE DOCUMENT

Authority *NLE* ~~TOP SECRET~~

By _____ NLE Date _9/1/78_

~~SECRET~~

October 29, 1962

MEMORANDUM OF TELEPHONE CONVERSATION

WITH PRESIDENT KENNEDY:

Yesterday, Sunday morning, President Kennedy called me on the phone to tell me about certain messages that he had received from Khrushchev dealing with the efforts to solve the Soviet-American differences in the Cuban situation. He did not quote to me the exact language of the messages that he had received from the Kremlin but did give their substance. The basic proposal was that Russia would dismantle all its bomb sites in Cuba if, in return, the United States would guarantee that it would not invade Cuba.

The messages received from the Russians contained different provisions but the final one seemed to be a very simple and, the President thought, quite acceptable in general intent. I concurred but told him that I thought our Government should be very careful about defining exactly what was meant by its promises. I observed, since we make a point of keeping our promises, that they should not imply anything more than we actually meant. It would be a mistake, I said, to give the Russians an unconditional pledge that we would, forever and under all conditions, not invade regardless of changing circumstances. For example, I said that if Castro should attack Guantanamo, or if he became active with agents and provocators in Latin American countries, it might become necessary for us to occupy the island.

My impression was that the President understood this and would make certain that we would not be over-committed. ...

I then called John McCone, head of the Central Intelligence Agency, who is normally my contact with the President on matters involving national security and gave him the gist of the conversation, particularly about the reservations that I thought should accompany any all-out promise of ours.

- more -

~~TOP SECRET~~

Memo dated October 29, 1962, of a telephone conversation with President John Kennedy about the Cuban missile crisis. Eisenhower was retired, but was still involved in national affairs.

South Vietnam, General William Westmoreland, all the support he requested. For Eisenhower, progress was too slow in Vietnam, and he thought it was due to Johnson's reluctance to use enough military force. He also disapproved of the large federal spending associated with Johnson's domestic programs.

In 1968 when Richard Nixon ran for president, Eisenhower endorsed him. Eisenhower had always had reservations about Nixon, who had been his vice-president. He thought Nixon needed more experience. He endorsed Nixon in 1968, because by then he had more respect for his ability.[6] By the time Nixon became president, Eisenhower's health was failing. He could no longer consult with Nixon as he had with Presidents Kennedy and Johnson.

In 1965 Eisenhower had a heart attack, his second. He knew that life was getting short, so he made preparations for his death. He had Ikky, his first son, who died in 1921, moved to the burial site that was planned for himself and Mamie. He suffered more heart attacks. With each one he became weaker. His friends and family could see that he was losing much of his energy. Still, he managed to enjoy life. He was happy about the marriage of his grandson David to President Nixon's daughter Julie in 1968. One biographer described how he enjoyed Thanksgiving dinner that year in the hospital with his family. Each member of the family ate part of the meal with him.[7]

In March 1969 he had another heart attack. By now

Eisenhower was very frail. He asked the well-known minister Billy Graham to visit him in the hospital. His family stayed close by, and again Mamie kept a room next to him. The end was getting close and Eisenhower knew it. On the day he died, his family was with him: Mamie, John, and his grandson David. He told Mamie that he had always loved her, their children, and grandchildren. "And I have always loved my country," he added.[8] The hardworking boy from Abilene, who had befriended the circus dog named Flip, said: "I want to go. God take me." He died on March 28, 1969.[9]

When Eisenhower left the White House, he experienced a sense of disappointment. He had wanted to reduce the suspicion between the two superpowers, the United States and the Soviet Union, but the situation now seemed worse. Despite his disappointment, he had made great strides in asserting American leadership. To begin with, his entry into politics grew out of his conviction that the political forces of isolationism must not prevail. Through the power of his personality, he tapped into his popular following and ended the question of America's role in global affairs. America became an even greater world leader while he was president. In view of world history since 1952, Eisenhower's belief in our country's international responsibility proved to be correct.

He managed to end the Korean War. Through his successful management of dangerous crises, so many that sometimes he dealt with two or more at once, he prevented other wars. Furthermore, throughout most of his first term, he had to cope with extremists, finding a way to keep peace during the peak years of the anti-Communist hysteria. He used patience and caution, often having to operate in the charged air of extremism. Yet he always accomplished his foremost goal, keeping the peace.

In a similar sense President Eisenhower accomplished much in the domestic arena. As an example, he resolved the question of "dismantling the New Deal." In other words, Eisenhower kept intact the basic structure of government reforms that went back to the 1930s. To be sure, he fought expansion of the government, but he also expanded social security benefits, maintained the agricultural support program, and started the federal highway construction program.

Civil rights was the only area where Eisenhower lacked strong leadership. Even though he is credited for the 1957 Civil Rights Act and for enforcing desegregation in Little Rock, Arkansas, in 1957, he refused to take a forceful stand on behalf of desegregation. Eisenhower was not, however, a segregationist. He was a constitutionalist on the subject of civil rights, meaning that he wanted desegregation to be handled by the courts. His job, he stated repeatedly, was to enforce the Constitution.

His critics regarded Eisenhower as an ineffective president. They claimed he was too grandfatherly—too old and not in control. In 1961, historians ranked him as only an average president.[10] As time progressed, however, the importance of his presidential leadership became clearer. By the 1980s his popularity among historians rose. They ranked him ninth among presidents in one poll. They stressed his success in quietly handling one crisis after another. They saw his role in ending Senator McCarthy's influence, and they appreciated his concern over military spending. His place in presidential history rose, in part, because of the release of documents by the Eisenhower Library. In another presidential poll taken in 1996, Eisenhower again ranked ninth.[11]

It has been more than thirty-five years since Eisenhower left office. If he had disappointments, he had achievements to counteract them. He is still remembered as the president who ended the Korean War which cost over fifty thousand Americans lives.

He is also fondly remembered for the prosperity of the 1950s, an era when the standard of living improved for most Americans. It was Eisenhower who balanced budgets and kept the peace during some of the most frightful years of the Cold War. And he was renowned for his honesty. When he left the White House, the presidency was an office of integrity because Dwight D. Eisenhower had been a man of integrity.

Chronology

1890—Born in Denison, Texas.

1891—Eisenhower family moves back to Abilene, Kansas.

1909—Graduates from high school.

1911—Enters West Point.

1915—Graduates from West Point.

1916—Marries Mamie Geneva Doud.

1917—First son, "Ikky" Doud Dwight, born.

1921—Death of Ikky.

1922—Second son, John Sheldon Doud, born.

1922—Serves under General Fox Conner in Panama
-1924   Canal zone.

1926—Graduates from Army Command School.

1929—Assigned to staff of Assistant Secretary of War.

1932—Participant in end of Bonus Army.

1933—Assigned to General Douglas MacArthur.

1935—Stationed in Philippine Islands with General MacArthur.

1939—Stationed at Fort Lewis, Washington.

1941—Organizes troop exercise in Louisiana.

1941—December 7: Japanese attack United States at Pearl Harbor.

1942—Assigned to staff of General George Marshall.

Made commander of Allied forces in North Africa.

1943—Made Supreme Allied Commander of forces in Europe.

1944—June 6: D-day battle. Invasion of Europe by Allies.

1945—World War II ends. Made Army Chief of Staff.

1948—Appointed president of Columbia University.

1951—Commander of North Atlantic Treaty Organization (NATO).

1952—Elected president of the United States.

1953—Korean War ended.

1950—Era of McCarthyism.
–1954

1954—First Formosa crisis. French forced out of Vietnam.

1955—First heart attack.

1956—Elected to second term as president. Suez crisis and Hungarian revolt.

1957—Integration of Little Rock high school. Russia launches *Sputnik*.

1958—Cuban revolution. Second Formosa crisis.

1960—*U-2* incident.

1961—Eisenhowers move to Gettysburg.

1969—March 28: Dies.

Chapter Notes

Chapter 1. D-day: The Battle of Normandy

1. David Eisenhower, *Eisenhower at War: 1943–1945* (New York: Random House, 1986), p. 251.

2. Ibid., pp. 170–171; Stephen E. Ambrose, *Eisenhower: Soldier-General of the Army, President-Elect, 1890–1952* (New York: Simon & Schuster, Inc., A Touchstone Book, 1983), p. 300.

3. Ambrose, p. 303.

4. Norman Gelb, *Ike and Monty: Generals at War* (New York: William Morrow and Company, Inc., 1994), p. 304.

5. Ambrose, p. 309.

6. Dwight D. Eisenhower, *Crusade in Europe* (Garden City, N.Y.: Doubleday & Company, Inc., 1948), p. 239.

7. Ibid.

8. Robert H. Ferrell, *The Eisenhower Diaries* (New York: W. W. Norton & Company, 1981), pp. 118.

9. Ibid., p. 118.

10. Eisenhower, *Eisenhower at War*, p. 272.

11. *The New York Times*, June 7, 1944, p. 10.

Chapter 2. Childhood and West Point, 1890–1915

1. Peter Lyon, *Eisenhower: Portrait of a Hero* (Boston: Little, Brown and Company, 1974), pp. 33–36; Steve Neal, *The Eisenhowers, Reluctant Dynasty* (Garden City, N.Y.: Doubleday Company, Inc., 1978), pp. 10–12.

2. Lyon, p. 37.

3. Dwight D. Eisenhower, *At Ease: Stories I Tell to Friends* (Garden City, N.Y.: Doubleday & Company, Inc., 1967), p. 67.

4. Ibid., p. 71.

5. Kenneth S. Davis, *Soldier of Democracy: A Biography of Dwight Eisenhower* (Garden City, N.Y.: Doubleday & Company, Inc., 1945), p. 77.

6. Eisenhower, *At Ease,* pp. 96–97.

7. For Eisenhower's own explanation of learning to play poker, see his book *At Ease,* pp. 89–90.

8. Davis, pp. 112–113.

9. Ibid., p. 134; Dwight D. Eisenhower, *IN REVIEW: Pictures I've Kept, A Concise Pictorial Autobiography* (Garden City, N.Y.: Doubleday & Company, Inc., 1969), p. 15.

10. Davis, pp. 136–137.

11. Eisenhower, *IN REVIEW,* p. 15.

12. Eisenhower had a temper. He argued with the math teacher about how to solve a problem. He was kept out of trouble only by the department chairman, who recognized that Ike had found an easier way to solve the problem than the teacher. Eisenhower later wrote that he had "an excellent chance of being expelled in disgrace from the Academy." See Eisenhower, *At Ease,* pp. 18–20; Jim Hargrove, *Encyclopedia of Presidents: Dwight D. Eisenhower, Thirty-Fourth President of the United States* (Chicago: Children's Press, 1987), p. 36.

Chapter 3. Military Career, 1915–1941

1. Susan Eisenhower, *Mrs. Ike: Memories and Recollections on the Life of Mamie Eisenhower* (New York: Farrar, Straus and Giroux, 1996), p. 34.

2. Kenneth S. Davis, *Soldier of Democracy: A Biography of Dwight Eisenhower* (Garden City, N.Y.: Doubleday & Company, Inc., 1945), pp. 161–162.

3. Eisenhower, *Mrs. Ike,* p. 51.

4. Stephen E. Ambrose, *Eisenhower: Soldier-General of the Army, President-Elect 1890–1952* (New York: Simon & Schuster, A Touchtone Book, 1983), pp. 64–65.

5. Ibid., pp. 70–71.

6. Eisenhower, *Mrs. Ike,* pp. 73–74.

7. Dwight D. Eisenhower, *IN REVIEW: Pictures I've Kept, A Concise Pictorial Autobiography* (Garden City, N.Y.: Doubleday & Company, Inc., 1969), p. 30.

8. Ambrose, p. 78.

9. Dwight D. Eisenhower, *At Ease: Stories I Tell to Friends* (Garden City, N.Y.: Doubleday & Company, Inc., 1967), pp. 198–203.

10. Ibid., pp. 210–212.

11. John D. Hicks, *Republican Ascendancy, 1921–1933* (New York: Harper Torchbooks, 1960), pp. 275–276; Peter Lyon, *Eisenhower: Portrait of a Hero* (Boston and Toronto: Little, Brown and Company, 1974), p. 69.

12. Donald J. Liso, *The President and Protest: Hoover, MacArthur and the Bonus Riot* (New York: Fordham University Press, 1994), p. 190; Joan Hoff Wilson, *Herbert Hoover: Forgotten Progressive* (Boston and Toronto: Little, Brown and Company, 1975), p. 161.

13. Eisenhower, *At Ease*, pp. 216–217.

14. Ibid., p. 220.

15. Ambrose, p. 108.

16. Eisenhower, *At Ease*, pp. 229–231.

17. Ibid.

18. Ambrose, pp. 120–132.

19. Davis, p. 276; Eisenhower, *At Ease*, p. 245.

20. Ibid., p. 230.

Chapter 4. World War II

1. Dwight D. Eisenhower, *At Ease: Stories I Tell to Friends* (Garden City, N.Y.: Doubleday & Company, 1967), p. 245.

2. Ibid., pp. 248–250; Stephen E. Ambrose, *Eisenhower: Soldier-General of the Army, President-Elect, 1890–1952* (New York: Simon & Schuster, 1983), pp. 133–144.

3. Robert F. Burk, *Dwight D. Eisenhower: Hero and Politician* (Boston: Twayne Publishers, 1986), p. 66; William B. Pickett, *Dwight D. Eisenhower and American Power* (Wheeling, Ill.: Harlan-Davidson, Inc., 1995), pp. 40–42; Alfred P. Chandler, ed. *The Papers of Dwight D. Eisenhower: The War Years II* (Baltimore and London: The Johns Hopkins Press, 1970), p. 739; Dwight D. Eisenhower, *Crusade in Europe* (Garden City, N.Y.: Doubleday & Company, 1948), pp. 95–112.

4. Burk, p. 66.

5. Ambrose, p. 210.

6. Kenneth S. Davis, *Eisenhower, American Hero: The Historical Record of His Life* (New York: American Heritage Publishing Co., Inc., 1969), pp. 45, 61–62.

7. David Eisenhower, *Eisenhower at War, 1943–1945* (New York: Random House, 1986), pp. 260–287.

8. Susan Eisenhower, *Mrs. Ike: Memories and Recollections on the Life of Mamie Eisenhower* (New York: Farrar, Straus and Giroux, 1996), p. 200.

9. Ibid., p. 207.

10. Eisenhower, *At Ease*, p. 291; Pickett, pp. 52–54; Eisenhower, *Crusade in Europe*, pp. 342–365.

11. Eisenhower, *At Ease*, p. 307.

12. Robert H. Ferrell, ed. *The Eisenhower Diaries* (New York: W. W. Norton and Company, 1981), p. 133; Alan Carpenter, *Dwight D. Eisenhower, The Warring Peacemaker* (Vero Beach, Fl.: Rourke Publications, Inc., 1987), pp. 64–66.

13. Ferrell, pp. 133–145.

14. Lester David and Irene David, *Ike and Mamie: The Story of the General and His Lady* (New York: G. P. Putnam's Sons, 1981), p. 171.

15. Douglas T. Miller and Marion Nowak, *The Fifties: The Way We Really Were* (Garden City, N.Y.: Doubleday & Company, Inc., 1977), pp. 21–30.

16. Ambrose, pp. 429–430.

17. Ferrell, p. 143.

18. *The New York Times*, July 11, 1948, p. 1.

19. Dwight D. Eisenhower, *IN REVIEW: Pictures I've Kept. A Concise Pictorial Autobiography* (Garden City, N.Y.: Doubleday & Company, Inc., 1969), pp. 108–110

20. Ambrose, p. 486.

21. Ibid., p. 464; Michael R. Beschloss, *Eisenhower: A Centennial Life* (New York: Edward Burlingame, 1990), p. 94.

22. Ferrell, p. 189.

23. Ibid., p. 186.

24. Herbert S. Parmet, *Eisenhower and the American Crusade* (New York: The Macmillan Company, 1972), pp. 45–56.

25. Ambrose, p. 523.

26. Burk, pp. 123–124.

27. Ibid., p. 125; Ambrose, p. 571.

Chapter 5. The Middle Way

1. Dwight D. Eisenhower, *Mandate for Change, 1953–1956* (Garden City, N.Y.: Doubleday & Company, Inc., 1963), p. 51.

2. Ibid.

3. Louis Galambos and Daun Van EE, eds., *The Papers of Dwight David Eisenhower, The Presidency: The Middle Way XIV* (Baltimore: The Johns Hopkins University Press, 1996), pp. xv–xx.

4. Stephen E. Ambrose, *Eisenhower: The President* (New York: Simon & Schuster, 1984), p. 199.

5. Robert Ferrell, ed., *The Eisenhower Diaries* (New York: W. W. Norton and Company, 1981), pp. 317–318.

6. Ambrose, p. 278.

7. William E. Leuchtenburg, *A Troubled Feast: American Society Since 1945* (Boston: Little, Brown and Company, 1973), p. 89; Eisenhower, pp. 287, 301–302.

8. Chester J. Pach, Jr., and Elmo Richardson, *The Presidency of Dwight D. Eisenhower* (Lawrence: University of Kansas Press, 1991), pp. 123–124.

9. Eisenhower, p. 83.

10. Ibid., p. 181.

11. David Halberstam, *The Fifties* (New York: Villard Books, 1993), pp. 49–59.

12. Eisenhower, p. 321.

13. Ferrell, p. 234.

14. Ambrose, p. 220.

15. Ibid., p. 249.

16. Eisenhower, pp. 484–487.

17. Ibid., p. 261; Martin J. Medhurst, "Eisenhower's Rhetorical Leadership: An Interpretation" in Martin J. Medhurst, ed. *Eisenhower's War of Words: Rhetoric and Leadership*, (East Lansing: Michigan State University Press, 1994), pp. 287–297.

18. Eisenhower, pp. 272–273.

19. Ambrose, p. 75.

20. Clarence G. Lasby, *Eisenhower's Heart Attack: How Ike Beat Heart Disease and Held on to the Presidency* (Lawrence: University Press of Kansas, 1997), pp. 293–332.

21. Douglas T. Miller and Marion Nowak, *The Fifties: The Way We Really Were* (Garden City, N.Y.: Doubleday & Company, Inc., 1977), p. 15.

Chapter 6. The Cold War: Atomic Attack?

1. Douglas T. Miller and Marion Nowak, *The Fifties: The Way We Really Were* (Garden City, N.Y.: Doubleday & Company, Inc., 1977), pp. 43–55.

2. Dwight D. Eisenhower, *Mandate for Change, 1953–1956* (Garden City, N.Y.: Doubleday & Company, Inc., 1963), pp. 459–460.

3. Ibid., p. 475.

4. Ibid., p. 464.

5. Ibid., p. 465.

6. Ibid., p. 482; William B. Pickett, *Dwight David Eisenhower and American Power* (Wheeling, Ill.: Harlan-Davidson, 1995), p. 124.

7. Eisenhower, *Mandate for Change*, p. 345.

8. Chester J. Pach, Jr., and Elmo Richardson, *The Presidency of Dwight D. Eisenhower* (Lawrence: University of Kansas Press, 1991), pp. 95–96.

9. Dwight D. Eisenhower, *Waging Peace, 1956–1961: The White House Years* (Garden City, N.Y.: Doubleday & Company, Inc., 1965), pp. 34–35.

10. Cole C. Kingseed, *Eisenhower and the Suez Crisis of 1956* (Baton Rouge: Louisiana State University Press, 1995), p. 74.

11. Eisenhower, *Waging Peace*, pp. 58–60.

12. Richard A. Melanson and David Mayers, eds., *Reevaluating Eisenhower: American Foreign Policy in the 1950s* (Urbana and Chicago: University of Illinois Press, 1987), p. 4.

13. Eisenhower, *Waging Peace*, p. 89.

14. Ibid., p. 80.

15. Ibid., p. 91; Kingseed, p. 118.

16. Ibid., p. 117.

17. Pach and Richardson, pp. 160–163.

Chapter 7. Keeping Peace in a Turbulent World

1. William J. Cooper, Jr., and Thomas E. Terrill, *The American South: A History, vol. 2* (New York: McGraw-Hill Companies, Inc., 1996), p. 688; Arthur Larson, *Eisenhower: The President Nobody Knew* (New York: Charles Scribner's Sons, 1968), p. 129; Donald W. Jackson and James W. Riddlesperger, Jr., "The Eisenhower Administration and the 1957 Civil Rights Act," in Shirley Anne Warshaw, ed., *Reexamining the Eisenhower Presidency* (Westport, Conn.: Greenwood Press, 1993), p. 98; "The Eisenhower Legacy in Civil Rights," in Shirley Anne Warshaw, ed., *The Eisenhower Legacy: Discussions of Presidential Leadership* (Silver Spring, Md.: Bartleby Press, 1992), pp. 64, 69.

2. Dwight D. Eisenhower, *Waging Peace, 1956–1961* (Garden City, N.Y.: Doubleday & Company, Inc., 1965), p. 164; Chester J. Pach, Jr., and Elmo Richardson, *The Presidency of Dwight D. Eisenhower* (Lawrence: University of Kansas Press, 1991), p. 150.

3. Ibid., p. 151.

4. Robert Griffith, ed., *Ike's Letters to a Friend, 1941–1958* (Lawrence: University of Kansas Press, 1984), p. 193.

5. Charles P. Roland, *The Improbable Era: The South Since World War II* (Lexington: University Press of Kentucky, 1975), p. 40.

6. Eisenhower, p. 151; Pach and Richardson, pp. 137–150.

7. *Time*, October 21, 1957, p. 21; Giles Alston, "Eisenhower: Leadership in Space Policy," in Shirley Anne Warshaw, ed., *Reexamining the Eisenhower Presidency* (Westport: Greenwood Press, 1993), pp. 103-119.

8. Ibid.; Robert A. Devine, *The Sputnik Challenge* (New York and Oxford: Oxford University Press, 1993), pp. 3–17.

9. Ibid., p. 71.

10. Eisenhower, p. 260.

11. Ibid., pp. 323–324; "Eisenhower at Gettysburg," in Shirley Anne Warshaw, ed., *The Eisenhower Legacy: Discussions of Presidential Leadership* (Silver Spring, Md.: Bartleby Press, 1992), pp. 119–120, 128–129.

12. William Stivers, "Eisenhower and the Middle East," in *Reevaluating Eisenhower: American Foreign Policy in the 1950s* (Urbana and Chicago: University of Illinois Press, 1987), p. 202.

13. Eisenhower, pp. 275, 290–291.

14. Ibid., p. 293; Pach and Richardson, pp. 195–196.

15. Stephen E. Ambrose, *Eisenhower: The President* (New York: Simon & Schuster, 1984), pp. 455, 569.

16. Peter J. Roman, *Eisenhower and the Missile Gap* (Ithaca and London: Cornell University Press, 1995), pp. 1–2.

17. Pach and Richardson, p. 216.

18. Eisenhower, p. 553.

19. Pach and Richardson, p. 220.

20. Thomas G. Patterson, *Contesting Castro: The United States and the Triumph of the Cuban Revolution* (New York: Oxford University Press, 1994), pp. 226–233.

21. Ibid., pp. 250–254.

22. Eisenhower, pp. 612–614.

23. Ibid., p. 614.

24. Richard A. Melanson and David Mayers, *Reevaluating Eisenhower: American Foreign Policy in the 1950s* (Urbana and Chicago: University of Illinois Press, 1987), pp. 53–54.

25. Eisenhower, p. 616.

26. Charles J. G. Griffin, "New Light on Eisenhower's Farewell Address" in Martin J. Medhurst, ed., *Eisenhower's War of Words: Rhetoric and Leadership* (East Lansing: Michigan State University Press, 1994), pp. 273–284.

Chapter 8. Retirement and Legacy

1. Stephen E. Ambrose, *Eisenhower: The President* (New York: Simon & Schuster, 1984), p. 643.

2. Lester David and Irene David, *Ike and Mamie: The Story of the General and his Lady* (New York: G.P. Putnam's Sons, 1981), pp. 215–221; Susan Eisenhower, *Mrs. Ike: Memories and Recollections on the Life of Mamie Eisenhower* (New York: Farrar, Straus and Giroux, 1996), p. 74ff.

3. Ibid., p. 308.

4. Ibid., p. 306.

5. Robert H. Ferrell, ed., *The Eisenhower Diaries* (New York: W. W. Norton & Company, 1981), p. 390; Ambrose, pp. 636–641.

6. William Bragg Ewald, Jr., *Eisenhower, The President: Crucial Days, 1951–1960* (Englewood Cliffs, N.J.: Prentice-Hall, Inc., 1981), pp. 308–314; Ambrose, pp. 666–667, 673.

7. Ibid.

8. Eisenhower, p. 314.

9. Ambrose, p. 675; David and David, p. 255.

10. Chester J. Pach, Jr., and Elmo Richardson, *The Presidency of Dwight D. Eisenhower* (Lawrence: University of Kansas Press, 1991), p. 237; William B. Pickett, *Dwight D. Eisenhower and American Power* (Wheeling, Ill.: Harlan-Davidson, 1995), pp. 189–190.

11. *Fort Worth Star-Telegram*, February 8, 1997, Section A, p. 16.

Further Reading

Ambrose, Stephen E. *Eisenhower: Soldier-General of the Army, President-Elect, 1890–1952.* New York: Simon & Schuster, 1983.

————. *Eisenhower: The President.* New York: Simon & Schuster, 1984.

Burke, Robert F. *Dwight D. Eisenhower: Hero and Politician.* Boston: Twayne Publishers, 1986.

Eisenhower, David. *Eisenhower at War, 1943–1945.* New York: Random House, 1986.

Eisenhower, Dwight D. *Crusade in Europe.* Garden City, N.Y.: Doubleday & Company, Inc., 1948.

————. *Mandate for Change, 1953–1956: The White House Years.* Garden City, N.Y.: Doubleday & Company, 1963.

————. *Waging Peace, 1956–1961: The White House Years.* Garden City, N.Y.: Doubleday & Company, Inc., 1965.

Eisenhower, Susan. *Mrs. Ike: Memories and Reflections on the Life of Mamie Eisenhower.* New York: Farrar, Straus & Giroux, 1996.

Ferrell, Robert H., ed. *The Eisenhower Diaries.* New York and London: W. W. Norton & Company, 1981.

Greenstein, Fred I. *The Hidden-Hand Presidency: Eisenhower as Leader.* New York: Basic Books, Inc., 1982.

Halberstam, David. *The Fifties.* New York: Villard Books, 1993.

Pach, Chester J., and Elmo Richardson, *The Presidency of Dwight D. Eisenhower.* Revised ed. Lawrence: University Press of Kansas, 1991.

Pickett, William B. *Dwight David Eisenhower and American Power.* Wheeling, Ill.: Harlan-Davidson, Inc., 1995.

Warshaw, Shirley, ed. *The Eisenhower Legacy: Discussions of Presidential Leadership.* Silver Spring, Md.: Bartleby Press, 1992.

————. *Reexamining the Eisenhower Presidency.* Westport, Conn.: Greenwood Press, 1993.

Places to Visit and Internet Addresses

Dwight D. Eisenhower Center and Library

S.E. Fourth Street
Abilene, Kansas 67410
(785) 263–4751

http://history.cc.ukans.edu

Eisenhower National Historic Site

97 Taneytown Road
Gettysburg, Pennsylvania 17325
(717) 334–1124

**Grolier Online Presents the
American Presidency**

http://www.grolier.com/presidents

Sunsite: Eisenhower Presidential Library

http://www.sunsite.unc.edu/lia/president/
eisenhower.html

University of California

http:// www.ucdavis.edu

Index